IN GOD'S ETERNAL PLAN

FORREST S. WEILAND

LAMPION HOUSE PUBLISHING, LLC
Navasota, Texas 77868
2026

The Church in God's Eternal Plan

Lampion House Publishing, LLC
P.O. Box 1295
Navasota, TX 77868
Website: http://lampionhousepublishing.com/

ISBN: 979-8-9918278-4-3 (softcover)

Editor: David Mappes (PhD, Dallas Theological Seminary) teaches courses in New Testament, Old Testament, hermeneutics, theological method, and theology at numerous schools. He is also the Founder / Director of Nobility and Knowability Truth Ministries and serves as the senior Content Editor for Lampion House Publishing. See publications and various conference papers at https://www.davidmappes.com/

Cover design by Ben Weiland
Interior Design/Formatting by Vickie Swisher, Studio 20|20

Printed in the United States of America

To my wife Sue
who has so faithfully supported and encouraged
my teaching and writing ministry,
and to my son Ben and his wife Marisa
who are a special blessing to me,
and to my little grandson Forrest
who is a new joy in my life.

CONTENTS

INTRODUCTION

In a previous book titled *The Vindication of Messiah on Earth: Tracing Jesus and His Kingdom from Genesis to Revelation,* I maintained that God's purposes for mankind, the earth, and his kingdom encompass much more than just his designs for the church. I argued that we who live in what is often referred to as *the church age* tend to be theologically myopic, viewing the church as the beginning and end-all of God's purposes. My reason for stating this was my observation that many believers fail to make a distinction between what God did in the past—particularly in and through the nation of Israel—with that which he is doing today in building his church, and with what he plans to do after the church is gone. But in pointing this out, I was not inferring that the church was anything less than the supreme purpose of God in this present age. The church, not Israel, encompasses the salvific work of God in the world today. Israel is still God's elect nation but is currently in a hiatus due to God's express purpose of building his church. The Lord will return to complete the promises he made to Abraham's descendants, but right now the church is center stage, and as such, she is taking part in his eternal plan and being prepared to meet her Lord. I have titled this book *The Church in God's Eternal Plan* because I want to address the topic of the uniqueness of the body of Christ, or to use a German term, the *Einzigartigkeit* of the church in the plans of God. It is imperative that every believer, every member of the body of Christ, understands God's wondrous miracle, the church, since we are part of it.

I will discuss some of the church's practical purposes, but the focus will be on its theological distinctives. We live in a very pragmatic age where theology is often looked at as impractical. Yet, theological truths must form the foundation upon which practical life is built. Otherwise, we too easily fall into error and sin. Having lived in Germany for thirteen years as a Bible and theology teacher and church planter, I can affirm that our German brothers and sisters admire the practicality of American Christianity. After several generations of destitute liberal theology, my experience was that they welcomed the more practical approach to ministry and life. Even in our own post-Christian culture, we are often warned not to be, as the saying goes, "so heavenly minded that we are of no earthly good." But the Apostle Paul does not seem to be worried about that. He actually called us to a more heavenly mindset when he wrote, "Set your mind on the things above, not on the things that are on earth" (Col 3:2). In this book, I hope to do just that as we consider the church in God's eternal plan.

PART I

The Theological Distinctions OF THE CHURCH

DEFINING THE CHURCH

The first question to ask and answer is, what is the church, and how would we define it? The New Testament Greek term for church is ἐκκλησία (*Ekklesia*). The word is comprised of two parts, the preposition "ἐκ" meaning *out of* and the noun κλῆσις meaning *invitation* or *call*. The word does not necessarily have a religious connotation unless the context so determines. For example, on one occasion the word was used in the book of Acts to refer to a secular political gathering, "So then, some were shouting one thing and some another, for the *assembly* was in confusion and the majority did not know for what reason they had come together" (Acts 19:32, see also vv. 39, 41). In that situation, the term was translated into English as assembly. The word Ekklesia was employed in the Septuagint (lxx), the Greek translation of the Old Testament, to describe God's people, Israel, as an assembly or congregation when they were called together in the wilderness. Luke mentions this in the book of Acts when referring to Moses and the people, "This is the one who was in the congregation in the wilderness together with the angel who was speaking to him on Mount Sinai, and *who was* with our fathers; and he received living oracles to pass on to you" (Acts 7:38). In that verse the term "congregation" is ἐκκλησίᾳ (Ekklesia). The word was also spoken by Jesus on the cross when he quoted Psalm 22, saying, "I will proclaim your name to my brethren, in the midst of the congregation I will sing your praise" (Ps 22:22; Heb 2:12).

When we come to the New Testament epistles, the word "church" most frequently refers to the assembled followers of Christ who gather in various geographical locations (Acts 8:1; Rom 16:1; 1 Cor 1:2; 2 Cor 1:1; Eph 1:1; Phil 1:1; Col 1:2; 1 Thess 1:1; 2 Thess 2:1; Rev 1:11). It is noteworthy that in all these cases, the word never refers to a building but rather to those who are followers of Christ and thus part of God's family. The word also has a more theological and technical sense when it specifies those who are called out of the world to be the people of God in this age, as well as in the age to come. This concept is reflected in Jesus' words to his disciples, "I chose you out of the world" (John 15:19). Those whom Jesus calls out of the world are brought into union with himself by the Holy Spirit through the new birth. Our Lord spoke to Nicodemus about the need for the new birth,

> Jesus answered and said to him, "Truly, truly, I say to you, unless one is born again he cannot see the kingdom of God" (John 3:3).

Theologically, the new birth involves regeneration, being born from above or from God by the Spirit (John 3:3, 5; 1 John 5:1). God causes us to be born again the moment we place our trust in Jesus and his death on the cross for our sins (1 Pet 1:3-5; Eph 2:8). This spiritual birth unites us forever to God through the Spirit.

> In Him, you also, after listening to the message of truth, the gospel of your salvation, having also believed, you were sealed in Him with the Holy Spirit of promise (Eph 1:13).
>
> In addition, the spiritual birth also unites believers to one another in a spiritual sense, so we, though many, are one body in Christ, and individually members one of another (Rom 12:5).
>
> . . . for we are members of one another (Eph 4:25).

Though the church has a physical manifestation on earth, in its essence, it is a supernatural spiritual organism. Whereas the local gatherings may include some non-believers, the universal church consists only of those who have been united to Christ through the Holy Spirit.

Thus, to summarize the general concept, "church," as it is used in the epistles, specifies groups of believers who gather in various geographical locations, whom God has called from the world to faith in his Son. From his position in heaven, outside of time, God summons them to salvation for the purpose of becoming part of his universal body. What is significant in this definition of church nowhere refers to what many people commonly think of today—a building or fabric of culture. Rather, it refers to those individuals who comprise the spiritual body of Christ.

GOD'S PEOPLE, THEN AND NOW: *DISTINGUISHING THE CHURCH FROM ISRAEL*

There has been and continues to be much debate as to whether the church has replaced the nation of Israel in God's plan. Yet almost all theological persuasions would admit that there are some distinctions between the two. Historically, Israel consists of the physical descendants of Abraham, descended first through Isaac and then through Jacob, and comprises just one nation. Some of these descendants of Abraham (Jews) have believed in Jesus as the Messiah, but most have not (cf. John 1:47; Rom 2:28; 9:6; Gal 6:16). By way of contrast, the church consists of individuals called from all nations of the world. When Jesus gave the Great Commission, he sent his followers into all the world to preach the gospel so that God could draw men and women to himself from every nation (Matt 28:19-20).

When this commission reaches completion, the church will be comprised of believers in the Messiah from every nation on earth, including Israel. We see a glimpse of the fulfillment of this reality in the book of Revelation. God is ruling from his throne in heaven (Rev 4–5). He holds a scroll secured with seven seals in his hand. The Lamb, who is Christ, is the only other being in heaven found worthy to break the seals of the scroll containing the judgments about to be poured out upon the earth (Rev 5:1-9). The living creatures and twenty-four elders declare that the Lamb had redeemed men and women from every nation of the earth,

> Worthy are You to take the book and to break its seals; for You were slain, and purchased for God with Your blood *men* from every tribe and tongue and people and nation (Rev 5:9).

This is one of the major distinctions between Israel and the church. Whereas the nation of Israel was limited to the descendants of Abraham through his grandson Jacob, the church encompasses believers from all nations. However, because of its faith in the Messiah, the church is identified as the spiritual descendants of Abraham,

> And if you belong to Christ, then you are Abraham's descendants, heirs according to promise (Gal 3:29).

That particular promise which the Apostle Paul cites was made to Abraham,

> And in you all the families of the earth will be blessed (Gen 12:3).

Thus, the church includes both Jews and Gentiles. Jews who believe in Christ as Messiah are both physical and spiritual descendants of Abraham (cf. Gen 12:2-3; 17:6-8; Num 23:9; Deut 7:6-8; 10:15-16; John 8:37; Gal 3:14, 16, 26-29). Gentiles who believe in Christ as Messiah are spiritual but not physical descendants of Abraham. In summary, Israel is one nation, the church is many.

There is yet another important distinction between Israel and the church. In the current age, every believer in Jesus, Jew or Gentile, is baptized into his body by the Holy Spirit. Paul writes,

> For by one Spirit we were all baptized into one body, whether Jews or Greeks, whether slaves or free, and we were all made to drink of one Spirit (1 Cor 12:13).

This spiritual work of the Spirit placing believers into one body, the body of Christ, did not occur with the people of God (the Jews and the proselyte Gentiles) prior to the pouring out of the Spirit in Acts 2. Although Old Testament believers (Jews and Gentiles) experienced salvation through faith and were no doubt regenerated by the Spirit, they were not baptized into one spiritual body, as believers are today (Gen 15:6; Hab 2:4).

When the church began in the book of Acts, the physical nation of Israel was seen as distinct from it. In the first decade, the church consisted primarily, if not solely, of Jewish believers (Acts 3:12; 4:10; 5:21, 31, 35; 21:28). Later Samaritans, and then Gentiles, became part of the body of Christ (Acts 8; 10). Yet, throughout the book of Acts, Luke distinguishes between the nation of Israel and the church. They exist simultaneously side by side. Never is Israel called the church, nor is the church called Israel. The term "Israel" referred to the nation comprised of ethnic Jews, and the church referred originally to believing Jews because they were the first believers to comprise the church. But later, once Gentiles began believing the gospel, the term referred to both believing Jews and Gentiles.

The term Israel occurs nineteen times in Acts and always refers to ethnic Israel. The term church occurs seventeen times in the same book. The first six of those occurrences are in Acts 5–11 when the church was still made up of primarily Jewish converts, and yet it remained distinct from Israel (the nation), which was mentioned seven times in those same chapters.

In addition to these distinctions, it is worth noting that the Abrahamic Covenant included a land grant, promised to the nation of Israel (Gen 12:1; 15:18-21; 17:8). No such promise was ever made to the church. Also, God promised Abraham physical descendants, which comprise the nation of Israel (Gen 12:2; 15:5; 22:17; 24:60; 26:4 32:12). No such promise of physical descendants was ever made to the church. These are some of the significant differences between ethnic Israel and the church. My point is that Israel and the church are distinct. They always have been. The Holy Spirit who inspired the Scriptures does not conflate or confuse the two.

Some expositors nevertheless maintain that the church has become the new Israel. They base their view partly on Paul's statement in Gal 6:15-16, which reads:

> For neither is circumcision anything, nor uncircumcision, but a new creation. And those who will walk by this rule, peace and mercy *be* upon them, and upon the Israel of God.

Some have used this verse to claim that the church is the "Israel of God." Paul's main point here is that in the era of the church, whether a person is physically circumcised or not does not matter, but what matters is that one has experienced the new birth. This, of course, applies to both Jews and Gentiles. Then he concludes the thought by saying to those who follow this teaching, "peace and mercy be upon them, and upon the Israel of God." Some interpreters have taken the plural pronoun "them" and the phrase "Israel of God" to refer to the same group, that is, the church. They translate the phrase as "peace and mercy be upon them, *even* the Israel of God" (emphasis mine). To arrive at this interpretation, the Greek conjunction *kai* must be translated as "*even*," making the two groups the same. Although *kai* can be translated as "even," that is the rare exception. Most often it is translated as "and." If we allow the more dominant translation of *kai*, then it seems likely that Paul was referring to (or distinguishing between) two groups, the first group being referred to as "them," that is the Galatian (Gentile) believers who followed Paul's teaching regarding the new creation, and a second group, the Jewish believers who are identified as "the Israel of God."

> Grace and mercy be *upon* them,
> and *upon* the Israel of God" (emphases added).

The repetition of the preposition "upon" in Gal 6:16 is not conclusive but lends some support to the interpretation that two groups are in view.

The designation "Israel" occurs more than seventy times in the New Testament. The word always refers to the Jewish people, so it would be highly unusual for this single occurrence to refer to the church. But even if one were to grant the view that the "Israel of God" refers to the church, it still would not mean that the church has replaced national Israel or that God has reneged on the promises he made to the physical descendants of Abraham, the Jewish people.

MESSIAH'S DEATH AND RESURRECTION, THE SEED OF THE CHURCH

God has not related to humanity in the same way throughout history. For example, he managed his relationship with Israel under the Mosaic Covenant differently than he manages his relationship with the church under the New Covenant. But salvation in every age has been based on the same divine provision, the death and resurrection of the Messiah. From the fall of man to the new heavens and earth, redemption has been founded upon the single provision made at the cross and appropriated through faith. This has been true for God's people in the past, and it is true for the church today. The New Testament writers describe this event in many ways. Jesus himself summarized it,

> unless a grain of wheat falls into the earth and dies, it remains alone; but if it dies, it bears much fruit (John 12:24).

Without Christ's death there would be no salvation, there would be no church. When the Son of God offered himself on the cross as an atoning sacrifice for our sins, his death paid the price which the righteousness of God demanded, satisfying his justice, averting his wrath, providing redemption and reconciliation (John 5:24; Rom 3:21-26; Col 1:20; 1 Thess 5:9; 1 Pet 1:18-19; John 2:2). All the benefits and blessings the church receives are founded upon and flow from the Messiah's passion (his suffering, death and burial), and his subsequent resurrection and ascension.

Although the sacrifice of the Messiah took place in history, it had been planned before time began (Acts 2:23; 4:28; 1 Pet 1:20; Rev 13:8). Its outworking was cosmic in scope because it became the provision whereby God would free the creation from corruption (Rom 8:20-22). Heaven itself needed to be cleansed from the effects of the fall (Heb 9:23-24). All things in heaven and earth needed to experience reconciliation:

> through Him to reconcile all things to Himself, having made peace through the blood of His cross; through Him, I say, whether things on earth or things in heaven (Col 1:20).

Regarding the church, his single sacrifice was the divine provision for its eternal life.

> I am the living bread that came down out of heaven; if anyone eats of this bread, he will live forever; and the bread also which I will give for the life of the world is My flesh (John 6:51).

> I am the good shepherd; the good shepherd lays down His life for the sheep (John 10:11).

CHRIST AS GOD'S MYSTERY

In the Old Testament, the Hebrew word for "mystery" רָז (*raz*) was used exclusively by the prophet Daniel. He employed the singular form six times (Dan 2:18, 19, 27, 30, 47; 4:9) and its plural three times (Dan 2:28, 29, 47). Daniel coined the word specifically to refer to the unknown contents of two separate dreams that King Nebuchadnezzar experienced. God was the one who made known the meaning of those dreams to the prophet Daniel. The prophet referred to them as mysteries because only God was able to divulge their content and meaning.

When we come to the New Testament, the Greek word for "mystery" (μυστήριον) and its plural "mysteries" (μυστήρια) are employed twenty-seven times.[1] When they are all considered, it becomes clear that they do not all refer to exactly the same thing, but they do appear to be interrelated and to overlap in their meaning. What is common to them all is that they com-

1 It is questionable whether Paul used the term μυστήριον "mystery" in 1 Cor 2:1. Most manuscripts have instead the word μαρτύριον, "testimony."

prise new revelations, that is, they unveil new truths or information about the subjects they address.[2] The content of these mysteries was at one time unknown and inaccessible to mankind, but then at a particular point in time God chose to unveil these mysteries or make them known to his people by means of revelation. These revelations consisted of truths that had not been known in the Old Testament period but were revealed in the New Testament era.

Christ himself is identified as God's mystery (Eph 3:3; Col 2:2; 4:3). In Col 2, Paul prays that the church would come to an understanding of,

> the true knowledge of God's mystery, *that is*, Christ *Himself* in whom are hidden all the treasures of wisdom and knowledge (Col 2:2).

In what sense is Christ God's mystery? We have defined or categorized the term "mystery" in the New Testament as referring to new revelations. But in what sense is Jesus a new revelation? Certainly, some things were already known about him in the Old Testament era. He is eternal and existed before and after the creation (John 1:1). At times, he appeared as the Angel of the Lord, the second person of the Trinity, taking on the form and role of God's messenger (Gen 18:1-33; Judg 13:2-23). In addition, it was known that the Messiah was prophesied to be born a human and of a virgin (Gen 3:15; Isa 7:14; Matt 1:23). So, if the second person of the Trinity existed and was known in

2 Those new revelations include: the mysteries of the Kingdom of God (Matt 13:11; Mark 4:11; Luke 8:10); the mystery of Israel's partial hardening (Rom 11:25); the mystery of the gospel (Rom 16:25; Eph 6:19; Col 4:3); the mystery of God's wisdom (1 Cor 2:7); the mysteries revealed through unknown tongues (1 Cor 14:2); the mystery of the translation of the Church (1 Cor 15: 50-58; see also 1 Thess 4:13-18; John 14:2-3); the mystery of God's will (Eph 1:9); the mystery of Christ (Eph 3:3; Col 2:2; 4:3); the mystery of the body of Christ and its administration (Eph 3:1-12); the mystery of Christ and the church (Eph 5:22-33); the mystery of Christ's indwelling (Col 1:24-29); the mystery of lawlessness (2 Thess 2:1-12); the mystery of the faith (1 Tim 3:9); the mystery of godliness (1 Tim 3:16); the mystery of the seven stars and seven golden lampstands (Rev 1:20); the mystery of God's eternal plan (Rev 10:7); and the mystery of Babylon the Great (Rev 17). Paul reveals that the apostles were stewards of the mysteries (1 Cor 4:1) and that knowledge of the mysteries was considered to be inferior to love (1 Cor 13:2).

the Old Testament era, in what sense was he a new revelation, or why is he referred to by Paul as a mystery?

It was not until the First Advent that the Messiah became flesh (John 1:14). It was not until the incarnation that God began to give a full and final revelation of himself through Jesus. Christ displayed a full or perfect revelation of God, the Father. In the prologue to his Gospel, John asserts that no one has ever seen God, but Jesus had "explained" him. Later in the same Gospel, Jesus, when speaking to Phillip, said, "He who has seen me has seen the Father" (John 1:18; 14:9). Later, in Col 1:15, the Apostle Paul reiterates this truth, "He is the image of the invisible God." In the next chapter Paul continues, "For in Him all the fullness of Deity dwells in bodily form" (Col 2:9). The author of Hebrews confirms this when he writes, "He is the radiance of His glory and the exact representation of His [God's] nature" (Heb 1:3). That a Messiah was to come was clearly understood in the Old Testament era and that he was to be human was perhaps understood by some, but the fullness of his divine nature and messianic office had not yet been fully unveiled. It was in his incarnation and earthly ministry that the deity and humanity of Christ were fully revealed. Of course, the only historical record of that incarnation is found in the New Testament, specifically the four Gospels, and the books that follow offer a divine commentary on that revelation. Jesus is God's mystery in the sense that he is the full revelation and manifestation of God. Before his incarnation, this revelation had not been fully disclosed.

THE CHURCH AS CHRIST'S MYSTERY

Closely connected to the mystery of Christ are God's purposes and plan for the church. The church itself is a mystery because of its spiritual union with Christ, who is designated as God's mystery. In Eph 3, the Apostle Paul refers to the church as one of the mysteries that God had revealed to him. He first mentions the mystery without defining it in verse 3, "by revelation there was made known to me the mystery, as I wrote before in brief." But then in verse 4, he states, "By referring to this, when you read, you can understand my insight into the mystery of Christ." Upon a cursory reading of this, one could easily conclude that Christ himself is the mystery, but as we read further, Paul goes on to specifically describe the mystery in verse 6,

> *to be specific*, that the Gentiles are fellow heirs and fellow members of the body, and fellow partakers of the promise in Christ Jesus through the gospel.

So when Paul refers to "the mystery of Christ" in verse 4, it seems likely that he is referring to a mystery that belongs to Christ or is sourced in him, or is so closely related to him that it is called by his name, "the mystery of Christ." That particular mystery was the truth that God, through his Spirit, had unified the Gentile and Jewish believers in Jesus into one new spiritual body, the church. Paul asserts,

> that by revelation there was made known to me the mystery, as I wrote before in brief. By referring to this, when you read you can understand my insight into the mystery of Christ, which in other generations was not made known to the sons of men, as it has now been revealed to His holy apostles and prophets in the Spirit; *to be specific*, that the Gentiles are fellow heirs and fellow members of the body, and fellow partakers of the promise in Christ Jesus through the gospel (Eph 3:3-6).

Though the Old Testament prophets did foresee a time when Gentile nations would travel to Israel to worship God (Isa 2:2-4; Zech 8:20-23), that phenomenon would not take place until after the second coming of the Messiah. That is not what Paul is referring to in Eph 3. The specific revelation that the church made up of both Jews and Gentiles would be unified in one spiritual body and have equal access to God lay hidden in the counsels of God until it was first revealed by Jesus when he stated, "I will build my church" (Matt 16:18).

It was to the Apostle Paul that God revealed the unique nature of the church as consisting of both Jews and Gentiles having equal access to God, something that was not true under the Law (Eph 2:18; 3:12; Heb 4:16). In the church every member is baptized into the body of Christ through a spiritual baptism that did not exist before the pouring out of the Spirit at Pentecost (Acts 2:1-4).

> For by one Spirit we were all baptized into one body, whether Jews or Greeks, whether slaves or free, and we were all made to drink of one Spirit (1 Cor 12:13).

This spiritual baptism into the body of Christ was a new miraculous work of God's Spirit. Another significant feature of the church is that each member is indwelt eternally by the Holy Spirit in contrast to the temporal empowering during the time under the Old Covenant. For example, when King Saul sinned, the Spirit departed from him, but for the believer today the Spirit's indwelling is forever.

> Now the Spirit of the LORD departed from Saul, and an evil spirit from the LORD terrorized him (1 Sam 16:14).

> I will ask the Father, and He will give you another Helper, that He may be with you forever; *that is* the Spirit of truth, whom the world cannot receive, because it does not see Him or know Him, *but* you know Him because He abides with you and will be in you (John 14:16-17).

Because of the unique work of the Spirit in the life of the believer in the body of Christ, there naturally results an intimate relationship between the Lord and each believer, and a spiritual kinship that unites all believers to one another. The church, then, is a new work of God, its newness being the union of Gentile believers with the Jewish believers in one body and the union of all believers with one another. Paul maintains that this new work did not exist in previous generations,

> the mystery of Christ, which in other generations was not made known to the sons of men, as it has now been revealed to His holy apostles and prophets in the Spirit (Eph 3:4b-5).

To the church today, which is largely comprised of Gentile (non-Jewish) believers, this revelation may seem unremarkable. But we should not forget that for more than two millennia, the chosen people of God were not from the Gentile nations but were strictly the Jewish people descended from Abraham that formed the nation of Israel. This continued up until after the death and resurrection of the Messiah and his sending of the Spirit to form the church at Pentecost. Although the church has not always existed, it was nevertheless in the eternal plan of God that he would bring to fruition at its appointed time. God revealed to the Apostle Paul that he had given him the particular responsibility of revealing this mystery to the church,

> To me, the very least of all saints, this grace was given, to preach to the Gentiles the unfathomable riches of Christ, and to bring to light what is the administration of the mystery which for ages has been hidden in God who created all things; so that the manifold wisdom of God might now be made known through the church to the rulers and the authorities in the heavenly *places. This was* in accordance with the eternal purpose which He carried out in Christ Jesus our Lord (Eph 3:8-11).

Several observations can be made on the above passage. First, the Apostle Paul understood that his responsibility of revealing this truth about the church was a gift of God's grace to him. Second, his particular task was to bring to light or to clarify the "administration" of the mystery. This refers to God's stewardship of the church, his plan and strategy for the church, first in human history and then into eternity. Third, this plan had been hidden in times past, "the mystery which for ages has been hidden in God." Fourth, the church itself was to be a vehicle of revelation to the angelic world, "to the rulers and the authorities in the heavenly *places*." Finally, this plan for the church is linked to the person of Christ. It was and is being carried out "in Christ Jesus."

Historically, the church began with the apostles and the small group of Jewish believers in Jerusalem, altogether numbering about 120 (Acts 1:12-15; 2:1-4). None of them were Gentiles. If a Gentile wanted to identify with and worship the God of the Bible, the God of the Jews, he or she would need to become a proselyte to Judaism. If they were males, they would undergo circumcision and adopt the Jewish law to the degree possible by making pilgrimages to the Jerusalem temple.

The uniqueness of the church in contrast to Israel is that Gentiles, along with believing Jews, were granted immediate and equal access to God and an equal standing before him. That would have been unthinkable under the Mosaic Covenant. Although Paul revealed this new mystery around AD 60 in his letter to the Ephesians, the revelation had been made known to him some years earlier. It may have been on the Damascus road (Acts 9:3-9) or in one of the other visions he experienced (Acts 22:17-18; 2 Cor 12:2-7; Gal 1:12).

Historically, a series of steps led to the incorporation of the Gentiles into the body of Christ, the church. First, there were those Jews at Pentecost who had gathered from "every nation under heaven" that heard the gospel. The result was that about "three thousand" of them came to faith in Christ as the Messiah (Acts 2:5, 41).

As the church grew, both native Jews and Hellenistic Jews were becoming part of the church (Acts 6:1). It was not until Acts 8 that a persecution scattered the believers from Jerusalem into the area of Samaria. Philip began proclaiming the gospel to the Samaritans, who were not full-blooded Gentiles nor full-blooded Jews. Beginning with the Assyrian captivity in 722 BC, Jews from northern Israel, the area of Samaria, were taken captive to Assyria, and Samaria was repopulated with peoples from Assyria (2 Kings 17:1-26). Over the years, the Jews who remained in Samaria began to intermarry with the Assyrians. The offspring from those marriages were called Samaritans (John 4). So, the Samaritans to whom Phillip preached were not full-blooded Jews but rather half-Jews. Peter and John followed up Philip's ministry by praying for the new Samaritan believers to receive the Holy Spirit, which they did, making them members of the body of Christ.

The first recorded full-blooded Gentile that responded to the gospel after Pentecost was the Ethiopian eunuch, who was apparently a proselyte to Judaism, for he had come to Jerusalem to worship God. After this, in Acts 10, another full-blooded Gentile named Cornelius, who was not a proselyte, came to faith in Christ as the Messiah. He was a God-fearer but not yet saved (cf. Acts 10:2; 11:14). During Peter's preaching of the gospel, the Holy Spirit came upon Cornelius, his relatives, and close friends. This revealed that God was not partial but gave full access to anyone, Jew or Gentile, who came to him through faith in his Son, Jesus Christ. So, the book of Acts demonstrates the historical process of incorporating all the major people groups into the body of Christ.

This new work of God was an unforeseen plan that "for ages had been hidden" in the eternal counsel of God (Eph 3:9). It was purposed in God's eternal wisdom, "predestined before the ages," that is, before world history began (1 Cor 2:7). Paul describes it as,

> the mystery which has been hidden from the *past* ages and generations, but has now been manifested to His saints (Col 1:26).

The new revelation was not that Gentiles would be saved, for that was clearly revealed in the Old Testament. The mystery or new revelation was that Gentiles would be granted direct access to and equal standing before God, along with the Jewish believers, through faith in the Messiah. Paul refers to this new work of God as "new man," something that had not previously existed.

> So that in Himself He might make the two into one new man, *thus* establishing peace (Eph 2:15b).

So, we can say that not only is Christ a mystery (or a new revelation), but so also is his new work, the church. The full extent of the mystery of the church becomes clearer as we look at other passages, particularly in Ephesians and Colossians, which describe it. In Eph 2, the apostle reminds the Gentile believers of their condition before their salvation,

> *remember* that you were at that time separate from Christ, excluded from the commonwealth of Israel, and strangers to the covenants of promise, having no hope and without God in the world (Eph 2:12).

This means that before they became part of the body of Christ, they had no relationship to the Messiah nor to the nation of Israel. They had not been a part of nor partaken in the major Old Testament covenants that God had made with Israel. God had indeed promised to Abraham that all nations would be blessed through him, but those nations had not yet experienced the promised blessing that would come through faith in the Messiah. But with the creation of the Jew-Gentile body of Christ, after his death, resurrection, ascension, and sending of the Spirit, this all changed.

> But now in Christ Jesus you who formerly were far off have been brought near by the blood of Christ. For He Himself is our peace, who made both groups [Jew and Gentile] *into* one and broke down the barrier of the dividing wall, by abolishing in His flesh the enmity, *which is* the Law of commandments *contained* in ordinances, so that in Himself He might make the two into one new man, *thus* establishing peace, and might reconcile them both in one body to God through the cross, by it having put to death the enmity. AND HE CAME AND PREACHED PEACE TO YOU WHO WERE FAR AWAY, AND PEACE TO THOSE WHO WERE NEAR; for through Him we both have our access in one Spirit to the Father (Eph 2:13-18).

These verses explain what was brought about by the unifying of Jews and Gentiles into one spiritual body. Clearly, it was made possible through "the blood of Christ." The cross brought the Gentiles who were, spiritually speaking, far away from God, near into the realm of his saving grace. The Gentile who believes enters the body of Christ and is at peace with the believing Jew who is also part of the same spiritual body. The former wall between the Jews and Gentiles was the Law, which had the effect of alienating the two groups. God effected this separation by giving Israel the Law for the purpose of keeping Israel distinct from the nations until the Messiah was brought into the world (Gal 3:19). In Christ, the Jews and Gentiles are reconciled into one group. Both groups now have equal standing before God and equal access to him. The result of this great work of God is expressed in the following verses:

> So then you are no longer strangers and aliens, but you are fellow citizens with the saints, and are of God's household, having been built on the foundation of the apostles and prophets, Christ Jesus Himself being the corner *stone*, in whom the whole building, being fitted together, is growing into a holy temple in the Lord, in whom you also are being built together into a dwelling of God in the Spirit (Eph 2:19-22).

Calling the Gentiles "fellow citizens with the [Jewish] saints," identifying them as the household of God, and having the same foundation as the Jewish believers reveals the perfect unity of the body of Christ. The two groups have become one dwelling place of God by means of His Spirit. This does not mean that the promises specifically made to the nation of Israel had been abrogated, but it did mean that God had begun a new work called the church.

Later in the same letter, when comparing the unity in marriage to the unity between Christ and his church, the apostle marvels at the greatness of this revelation,

> 'For this reason a man shall leave his father and mother and shall be joined to his wife, and the two shall become one flesh.' This mystery is great; but *I am speaking with reference to Christ and the church* (emphasis mine, Eph 5:31-32).

The centuries of enmity that had been built up between Jews and the Gentiles had been defused by the cross in which Jesus reconciled the Jew and Gentile into one body through faith in him. All of this is subsumed under the concept of "mystery" because it was a new revelation and a new work of God in salvation history.

THE ETERNAL ELECTION AND PREDESTINATION OF THE CHURCH

Election

Although this marvelous spiritual entity called the church had an organic starting point in human history, it is also true that the plan for the church existed eternally, before time, in the mind and purpose of God. When Paul referred to the church as being a revelation of God to the angelic world, he also indicated that it was a part of God's plan from eternity past.

> *This was* in accordance with the eternal purpose which He carried out in Christ Jesus our Lord (Eph 3:11).

This means that prior to Christ's promise to build the church (Matt 16:18) and before its establishment on earth (Acts 2), God had planned in eternity past to bring the church into being.

> He chose us in him before the foundation of the world (Eph 1:4).

In another letter the Apostle Paul confirms this point when he states that salvation, "was granted us in Christ Jesus from all eternity" (2 Tim 1:9).

Several New Testament passages confirm the truth of divine election.[3] Though some object to this doctrine, apart from it no one could be saved. Every man and woman born since Adam have been part of the fallen creation (Rom 3:23; 5:12). Because of his depravity, man is unable of himself to change the condition of his lostness. Thus, left to their own devices, humans do not and will not naturally seek the one true living God (Rom 3:10-13). They may seek another god or religion but not the God of the Bible. From the time of Adam and Eve's fall, there has

---

3 Other New Testament passages testify to the biblical doctrine of election: John 15:16, 19; Acts 13:48; Rom 8:29-30; 11:7; Eph 1:4; 2 Thess 2:13; 2 Tim 2:10; Tit 1:1; 1 Pet 1:1; 2:9; 5:13; 2 Pet 1:3.

been a natural bent in every human heart away from God (Rom 3:10). For this reason, if any are going to be rescued from judgment, God must initiate and complete this work of salvation. That work began in eternity past when God chose for himself those who would become recipients of his glorious salvation. This truth does not rule out the necessity of human choice, responsibility, and faith. For salvation to be actualized, a person must believe on the Messiah (John 8:24; Acts 16:31). But, for this to happen, the Spirit of God must convict or convince men that they are lost, in need of a savior, and that God has provided one in Jesus Christ (John 16:8; Rom 3:23). God must then draw rebellious men and women to himself and grant to them faith through which they obtain eternal life (John 6:44; 12:32; Eph 2:4-5, 8). Therefore, if any person is seeking the true God, it is because God the Holy Spirit is drawing them in that direction.

The sphere of God's election is expressed as "in him," that is, in Christ. Although election is individual, the phrase "in him" makes clear that it is in coordination and in union with God's purpose for the Messiah. This choice was not due to the believer's works or the believer's choice of God, but for a future purpose that God has with Christ and his church (John 15:16; Eph 5:27). "In Christ" each believer has received incalculable spiritual favor,

> Blessed *be* the God and Father of our Lord Jesus Christ, who has blessed us with every spiritual blessing in the heavenly *places* in Christ (Eph 1:3).

Part of this blessing is that we have been united to Christ in his death, burial, resurrection, and ascension. Galatians 2:20 states that we have been crucified with Christ, indicating that we have been spiritually united with him in his death. Romans 6:4 confirms this by saying that we have been "buried with Him through baptism into death." Colossians 3:1 says that we "have been raised up with Christ," pointing to the reality that the believer also shares in the Messiah's resurrection life. In addition, the believer has been "raised up with Him and seated with Him" in the heavenly places, demonstrating that we also share positionally in his ascension (Eph 2:6). In another passage, Paul emphasizes that the very power that raised Christ from the dead and transported him to heaven energizes the believer's life of faith.

> I pray...that you will know...what is the surpassing greatness of his power towards us who believe. *These are* in accordance with the working of the strength of His might which He brought about in Christ, when He raised Him from the dead and seated Him at His right hand in the heavenly *places*, far above all rule and authority and power and dominion, and every name that is named, not only in this age but also in the one to come (Eph 1:19-21).

In addition to these magnificent spiritual blessings that the church now experiences, there is the promise that we will in the future "*obtain* an inheritance *which* is imperishable and undefiled and will not fade away, reserved in heaven" (1 Pet 1:4). All of this is wrapped up in the grace and mercy of divine election.

Some people contend that the election of some individuals to salvation—but not all—is unjust and unfair. From the perspective of fallen man, this may seem to be the case, but the Bible clearly teaches that God is absolutely holy and just, and in Him is no darkness at all (1 John 1:5). God was in no way obligated or morally impelled to choose anyone to eternal life. His decision not to choose everyone does not in any way impinge upon his holy and righteous character, let alone his right as the sovereign God (Rom. 9:13-21). On the contrary, justice would demand that all receive the punishment they have rightly earned for their sins (Rom. 3:23; 6:23). Therefore, the question is not, why did God not choose all, but why did he choose any, when they all deserved judgment? God's election of some to salvation was grounded purely in his mercy, grace, and love, which he decided to lavish upon some despite their rebellion (Eph 1:4). God's holiness required that he provide for the cleansing of their sin, which he accomplished through the sacrifice of his beloved Son, Jesus Christ (Acts 2:23).

Predestination

Linked to the election of the church is its predestination. The term means to determine or decide something beforehand. Some form of the word occurs six times in the New Testament (Acts 4:28; Rom 8:29, 30; 1 Cor 2:7; Eph 1:5, 11). It is practically synonymous with the concept of foreordination and closely related to divine foreknowledge (Acts 2:23; Rom 8:29; 1 Pet 1:1-2, 20). God the Father is the one who predestines (John 17:6-10; Rom 8:29; Eph 1:3-5; 1 Pet 1:2).

> He predestined us to adoption as sons through Jesus Christ to Himself, according to the kind intention of His will...having been predestined according to His purpose who works all things after the counsel of His will (Eph 1:5, 11).

The secondary goal in predestination is that his elect, the church, becomes "holy and blameless before him in love" (Eph 1:4; 5:27). But the ultimate end of this magnificent work of God's grace is his honor and glory (Eph 1:4-6, 12). This means that God initiated the process of salvation by deciding that he wanted a certain number or group of people to appear before him as holy and blameless for the express purpose of demonstrating his glory. The decision to predestine some individuals to salvation was not based upon anything good or bad in the recipients but rather it was based solely in God's good pleasure and according to his holy, wise, and eternal purpose (Ps 33:11;

Isa 46:10; Acts 13:48; Rom 11:33). Those whom God has chosen are predestined in view of the purpose he desires to fulfill in them, that of becoming his children conformed to the image of his son (Rom 8:29). The ultimate purpose behind this plan is to bring glory to God (Eph 1:5-6, 11-12).

Election and predestination are parts of God's all-encompassing eternal plan (Isa 40:13-14; Rom.11:34; Eph 1:11). Several terms are employed to express this plan, among them are his "decree" (Ps 2:7), his "eternal purpose" (Eph 3:11), his "foreknowledge" (Acts 2:23), and his "will" (Eph 1:9, 11). Biblical writers inform us that God's sovereignty extends to all things that come to pass, including major and insignificant events, direct and indirect causes, things appointed, and things permitted. It therefore encompasses both good and evil (Ps 139:16; Prov 16:4; Isa 14:24-27; 22:11; 37:26-27; 46:9-10; Acts 2:23; 4:27-28; Eph 1:11; 2:10). The inclusion of evil under the rubric of God's sovereignty does not mean that he condones, authorizes, or commits moral evil. As noted above, the Apostle John stresses that God is light and that there is no darkness in him at all (1 John 1:5). He is absolutely holy and cannot be charged with the commission of sin, "*Your* eyes are too pure to approve evil, and you cannot look on wickedness *with favor*" (Hab 1:13).

When addressing the topic of God's plan and purpose, the biblical authors are careful to distinguish between divine causation and human responsibility. Both fall under the purview of God's sovereignty. There is divine certainty about what will happen, but moral agents are never under compulsion to commit evil, nor are our actions deterministic or mechanistic in the sense that God impels or forces us to do something and does not allow for the exercise of our own wills (see Acts 4:28; 1 Cor 2:7; Acts 26:5; Rom 9:11; 11:2; 1 Pet 1:2, 20; 2 Pet 3:17; Heb 2:5, 10-16). For example, when Luke refers to the greatest miscarriage of justice in the history of the world, the crucifixion of Christ, he indicates that it was predestined by God, but the moral turpitude of the act is attributed to "wicked men" (Acts 2:23). The dual nature of such events is aptly reflected in Joseph's statement to his brothers who sold him into slavery, "You meant it for evil, but God meant it for good" (Gen 50:20). Our understanding will not take us beyond this. We must humbly admit that how God works out all things is an inscrutable mystery to us.

Whereas the all-encompassing plan of God relates to his sovereign control over all things, predestination appears to be restricted primarily to certain divine decisions affecting humans, angels, and the Messiah (Isa 42:1-7; Acts 2:23; 1 Tim 5:21; 1 Pet 1:20; 2:4). With reference to humans, Paul states,

> In Him we were also chosen, having been predestined according to the plan of him who works out everything in conformity with the purpose of his will (Eph 1:11).

It appears that in his plan, God has chosen some individuals, nations, groups, and angels to fulfill special purposes. This infers that other individuals, groups, nations, or angels have not been selected for those same purposes (1 Pet 1:2; 2 Tim 2:10; 2 Thess 2:13). This has led some theologians to erroneously conclude that those not predestined for salvation are by default chosen for eternal damnation. They maintain that predestination applies not only to individuals whom God plans to save, but also to those whom he does not save. Several passages are usually cited to support this idea (Prov 16:4; Matt 26:23-24; Rom 9:10-13, 17-18, 21-22; 2 Tim 2:20; 1 Pet 2:8; 2 Pet 2:3, 9; Jude 4; Rev 13:8; 20:15). This is sometimes called "reprobation." The belief in the combined concepts of election and reprobation has been referred to as "double predestination." While some scholars in the history of the church have argued that God is just as active in determining the destiny of reprobate as he is the elect, others have pointed out that there is a distinct difference between

God's involvement in the two destinies. God's condemnation of the non-elect is based upon their sin and unbelief, not upon a pre-determined damnation (John 8:24). A real distinction exists in the level of divine causation with regard to the destiny of one class as compared with the other. God does not appear to have the same relationship to every event, thing, or person in his creation. Also, Scripture recognizes a difference between God's direct working and his permissive will. In this view, God directly chooses some to be saved, but he does not *choose* the others to be damned, but rather allows them to continue their own self-determined way, eventually suffering the just punishment their sins deserve. Thus, Scripture does not appear to teach reprobation in exactly the same way it teaches predestination unto eternal life. Whereas the assignment to eternal death is a judicial act taking into account man's sin, predestination unto eternal life is purely an act of God's sovereign grace and mercy not taking into account any actions good or evil by those chosen and predestined (Eph 2:4-8; Rev 20:12). Carrying the teaching of reprobation to the extreme threatens to view God as capricious which is clearly unscriptural (1 John 1:5).

Some theologians have argued that election and predestination are merely based upon God's foreknowledge of those who will believe in him. Although God surely knows all those who will believe, the term "foreknowledge" connotes much more than simply knowing ahead of time who will come to faith. It means that God has sovereignly chosen to know some individuals in such an intimate way that it moved him to predestine them to eternal life (Rom 8:29). Whereas election refers to God's sovereign choice of those individuals, predestination looks forward to the goal of that selection. Both predestination and election occurred before the creation of the world and were motivated by divine love (Eph 1:4-5; 3:11).

THE CHURCH: THE GIFT OF THE FATHER TO HIS SON

In this salvific work of creating the church, Jesus makes clear in the Gospel of John that his Father was preparing a gift for his Son. Notice in the following verses that the Father is giving something (believers) to the Son:

> All that the Father gives Me will come to Me, and the one who comes to Me I will certainly not cast out (John 6:37).
>
> even as You gave Him authority over all flesh, that to all whom You have given Him, He may give eternal life (John 17:2).
>
> I have manifested Your name to the men whom You gave Me out of the world; they were Yours and You gave them to Me" (John 17:6).
>
> I ask on their behalf; I do not ask on behalf of the world, but of those whom You have given Me; for they are Yours (John 17:9).
>
> Father, I desire that they also, whom You have given Me, be with Me where I am (John 17:24).

The gift that the Father is giving the Son is the church, which is comprised of those individuals selected by God in His eternal plan.

THE SEALING OF THE BELIEVER

The Apostle Paul mentions in three different verses that those who belong to the body of Christ, the church, have been "sealed."

> Now He who establishes us with you in Christ and anointed us is God who also sealed us and gave *us* the Spirit in our hearts as a pledge (2 Cor 1:21-22).
>
> In Him, you also, after listening to the message of truth, the gospel of your salvation—having also believed, you were sealed in Him with the Holy Spirit of promise (Eph 1:13).
>
> Do not grieve the Holy Spirit of God, by whom you were sealed for the day of redemption (Eph 4:30).

The significance of this sealing is practically identical to what is called the security of the believer. The Spirit is the One who seals. The seal is the spiritual protection given by God to assure that the believer will arrive safe in heaven in God's presence. The Apostle Peter refers to believers as those "who are protected by the power of God through faith for a salvation ready to be revealed in the last time" (1 Pet 1:5). This guarantee does not mean that a believer cannot fall into sin or temporarily fall away from Christ. What it does mean is that any defection will be disciplined and the believer restored in God's own time (Heb 12:5-8). A good example of this was the Apostle Peter in contrast to Judas. Peter was restored after denying Christ three times (Matt 26:69-75; John 21:15-19). Judas, after betraying Christ, was not restored (Matt 27:3-5; Acts 1:15-20). Although the believer's salvation is protected by the power of God, it is through faith not apart from it (1 Pet 1:5). The believer's faith must and will continue until he or she arrives safe in heaven (Heb 10:39). If the faith of any person does not endure, it merely reveals that it was not a saving faith but a defective one (Jas 2:14-26; 1 John 2:19). In some severe cases of sin by genuine believers, God may even bring discipline by death, taking the believer preemptively to heaven (1 Cor 11:30-32). But even in such cases, the believer's salvation is protected (1 Cor 3:15; 5:5; Jude 23).

THE MYSTERY OF CHRIST'S INDWELLING

Related to the mystery of the church is the mystery of Christ's indwelling. Paul describes this as "Christ in you, the hope of glory" (Col 1:26). As with the other mysteries, it involves a new revelation, one that had not been made in the past ages, during the period of the Old Testament.

> *that is*, the mystery which has been hidden from the *past* ages and generations, but has now been manifested to His saints, to whom God willed to make known what is the riches of the glory of this mystery among the Gentiles, which is Christ in you, the hope of glory (Col 1:26-27).

The mystery of Christ's indwelling pertains to Jesus taking up residence in his church as a whole and in each member individually. During the Old Testament period, there were instances in which the Spirit of God entered a person and filled him, ostensibly for a temporary period of time and for specific tasks. For example, God said of Bezalel, who was a man from the tribe of Judah, "I have filled him with the Spirit" (Exod 31:2-3). Also of Joshua, God said, "in whom is the Spirit" (Num 27:18). The prophet Ezekiel said of himself, "the Spirit entered me." Of Daniel, it was said by Nebuchadnezzar, Belshazzar, and the queen mother that the spirit of the gods or possibly the Spirit of God was in him (Dan 4:8, 9, 18; 5:11-14). At times, the Spirit's work was described as coming "upon" a person. For example, when Samson was traveling to Timnah, he was attacked by a lion, and the text says, "The Spirit of the Lord came upon him mightily, so that he tore him as one tears a young goat though he had nothing in his hand" (Judg 14:6). In these cases, the Spirit came upon select individuals, not all Israelites, and it was for a temporary period, enabling them to carry out special tasks or ministries. The temporal nature of God's indwelling or empowerment at that time was seen in the life of King Saul. God removed the

Spirit from Saul when he had sinned grievously against God (1 Sam 16:14). After David sinned with Bathsheba, he repented and prayed that God would not take his Holy Spirit from him as he had taken it from Saul. This showed that the Spirit's indwelling or equipping ministry was temporary. By way of contrast, God began an entirely new work at Pentecost, when he sent his Spirit into the world to permanently indwell and gift the church, namely, every believer. In the Gospel of John, Jesus announced the Spirit's future coming several times. On the last day of the Feast of Tabernacles, he declared,

> If anyone is thirsty, let him come to Me and drink. He who believes in Me, as the Scripture said, "From his innermost being will flow rivers of living water" (John 7:37-38).

The Gospel writer then explained what the living waters referred to,

> But this He spoke of the Spirit, whom those who believed in Him were to receive; for the Spirit was not yet *given*, because Jesus was not yet glorified (John 7:39).

It is clear in the above verse that the Spirit would not be given until after the death, resurrection, and ascension of Jesus. Later in John's Gospel, in the upper room during the last supper, Jesus again reminded the disciples that he would soon be sending the Holy Spirit to indwell them.

> I will ask the Father, and He will give you another Helper, that He may be with you forever *that is* the Spirit of truth, whom the world cannot receive, because it does not see Him or know Him, *but* you know Him because He abides with you and will be in you (John 14:16-17).

Perhaps most significant for this discussion is the last phrase, "He abides with you and will be in you." The distinction is between the Spirit being "with you" and the Spirit being "in you." In the Old Testament era, the Spirit was "with" or "in" select individuals for a temporary period of time, but after Pentecost the Spirit began to indwell every believer "forever." The pouring forth of the Spirit at Pentecost as recorded in Acts 2 marked the beginning of the church which Jesus had foretold in Matt 16:16-19.

The Apostle John made clear that the Holy Spirit would indwell each believer when he wrote, "if anyone is thirsty, let him come to Me and drink," but he also alludes to the corporate indwelling of the Spirit when he employs the plural "you" in "he will be with you forever" (cf. John 7:37-39). Paul also referred to the indwelling of the Spirit in the corporate sense or in the church as a whole. For example, he writes to the Corinthians,

> Do you not know that you are a temple of God and *that* the Spirit of God dwells in you?" (1 Cor 3:16).

The pronoun "you" (οἴδατε) is plural in the Greek text, indicating that he is referring to the church as a whole. He repeats this point a couple of chapters later, again using the plural pronoun "you."

> Or do you not know that your body is a temple of the Holy Spirit who is in you, whom you have from God, and that you are not your own?" (1 Cor 6:19).

Paul combines the concept of the Spirit indwelling the universal church as well as the individual believer in Rom 8:9,

> However, you are not in the flesh but in the Spirit, if indeed the Spirit of God dwells in you. But if anyone does not have the Spirit of Christ, he does not belong to Him.

In that verse, Paul used the plural pronoun "you" twice but then referred to "anyone." That would refer to each individual having the Spirit.

As new believers are added to this temple, it expands but remains unified as God's dwelling place.

> In whom the whole building, being fitted together, is growing into a holy temple in the Lord, in whom you also are being built together into a dwelling of God in the Spirit (Eph 2:21-22).

When Paul refers to the whole building being fitted together in the above passage, he is referring to the addition of each individual believer to the body of Christ. The apostle reveals the miraculous nature of this fitting together of the temple of God when he writes,

> For by one Spirit we were all baptized into one body, whether Jews or Greeks, whether slaves or free, and we were all made to drink of one Spirit" (1 Cor 12:13).

So, it is the supernatural work of the Spirit that places each believer into the body of Christ, the church. This is called a "mystery" because it was a revelation concerning a new work of God in which the Holy Spirit would indwell his church forever, and each member individually (Col 1:26).

One of the practical purposes of Christ's indwelling, as well as the indwelling of his Spirit, is to produce practical sanctification in the life of the believer.

> For this is the will of God, your sanctification (1 Thess 4:3).

The writer of Hebrews clarifies that Christ's death was the foundation of God's work of sanctification in the life of the believer,

> For by one offering He has perfected for all time those who are sanctified (Heb 10:14).

Yet, the believer is also called upon to participate in this progressive work,

> And everyone who has this hope *fixed* on Him purifies himself, just as He is pure (1 John 3:3).

> Therefore, having these promises, beloved, let us cleanse ourselves from all defilement of flesh and spirit, perfecting holiness in the fear of God (2 Cor 7:1).

In both the verses above, the believer, not God, is called upon to purify and cleanse him- or herself. The Apostle Paul explains how we engage in this ministry of self-purification:

> Even so consider yourselves to be dead to sin, but alive to God in Christ Jesus. Therefore, do not let sin reign in your mortal body so that you obey its lusts, and do not go on presenting the members of your body to sin *as* instruments of unrighteousness; but present yourselves to God as those alive from the dead, and your members *as* instruments of righteousness to God. For sin shall not be master over you, for you are not under law but under grace (Rom 6:11-14).

The function and goal of Christ's indwelling is to sanctify and transform us so that we might become more like him.

> But we all, with unveiled face, beholding as in a mirror the glory of the Lord, are being transformed into the same image from glory to glory, just as from the Lord, the Spirit (2 Cor 3:18).

THE UNITY OF CHRIST'S CHURCH

Believers often lament that the church throughout its history has fallen so short of the unity that Christ envisioned in his prayer in John 17. They point to the historical event of the Protestant Church breaking off from the Catholic Church at the time of the Reformation, and to the multitude of Protestant churches that have subsequently split and/or distinguished themselves along denominational lines. It cannot be denied that divisions and denominational distinctions abound. The church appears in many ways to be fragmented. Let's consider what Jesus prayed in John 17,

> I do not ask on behalf of these alone, but for those also who believe in Me through their word; that they may all be one; even as You, Father, *are* in Me and I in You, that they also may be in Us, so that the world may believe that You sent Me (John 17:20-21).

The first thing to note is that the unity for which Jesus prayed was supernatural because he compared it to the unity that existed between the Father and himself, "One; even as You, Father, are in Me and I in You." Has this type of unity been achieved, or is it something that is yet to come?

In his first letter, the Apostle John promised that if we ask anything according to God's will, he will answer (1 John 5:14). Jesus, being the second person of the Trinity, the Son of God, always prayed according to God's will. Even in Gethsemane he prayed, "Yet not as I will, but as You will (Matt 26:39). In John 17, he asked for the church to be one as he and the Father were one. There is one way to see that the Father has answered this request for unity. Shortly after the resurrection, after Jesus returned to heaven, on the Day of Pentecost recorded in Acts 2, he sent the Holy Spirit to indwell the church. The Holy Spirit began the ministry of taking up residence in the heart of every believer

(Rom 8:9). In addition, every believer was united to Christ and to his body through what is called the baptism of the Spirit (1 Cor 12:13). So, the Holy Spirit indwells every genuine believer and every believer has been placed into the body of Christ. Since it is one body, we are spiritually united to one another. Every genuine believer, from every generation since Pentecost in Acts 2, no matter what country they derive from, no matter what denomination they belong to, is united to Jesus and to one another (as the universal church). That is a unity we cannot undo or destroy, but it is also a unity we are called upon to preserve and protect in the bond of peace (Eph 4:3). So, to conclude this thought, though the church may not be unified in its outward manifestation in the world, it nevertheless does experience a union through the Spirit. In addition, the fulfillment of Jesus' prayer in John 17 may await the church's transport to heaven. It may be that when the church is gathered to be with Christ in heaven, then perfect unity will have been achieved.

CHRIST, THE HEAD OF THE BODY

If the church is known both spiritually and metaphorically as a body, it is only natural that such a body has a head. Christ himself exists as the head of that body. The Apostle Paul expresses it this way,

> He is also head of the body, the church (Col 1:18a).

This headship conveys leadership and authority over the church. More fundamentally, it expresses the organic unity that Christ has with every member of his church. Just as our physical head, containing the mind, controls and directs every member of our physical body, so Christ indwells every member of his body in a vital, empowering union. Paul expresses this truth in his letter to the Ephesians,

> And He put all things in subjection under His feet, and gave Him as head over all things to the church, which is His body, the fullness of Him who fills all in all (Eph 1:22-23).

The spiritual life of the body of Christ is sustained and supported by abiding in Christ, that is, remaining in vital union with him.

> Abide in Me, and I in you. As the branch cannot bear fruit of itself unless it abides in the vine, so neither *can* you unless you abide in Me. I am the vine, you are the branches; he who abides in Me and I in him, he bears much fruit, for apart from Me you can do nothing (John 15:4-5).

Although abiding is a command and therefore we play a role in obeying that command, it is also true that abiding is portrayed as something permanent. For example, God's Spirit in us causes us to abide (1 John 2:27; 4:13) as does our faith in Christ (1 John 4:15). The fact that he abides in us and we in him permanently forms the basis for the command for us to abide temporally. The organic growth of the body takes place through this union with Christ as the head, and the members with one another:

> but speaking the truth in love, we are to grow up in all *aspects* into Him who is the head, *even* Christ, from whom the whole body, being fitted and held together by what every joint supplies, according to the proper working of each individual part, causes the growth of the body for the building up of itself in love (Eph 4:15-16).

The work of Christ in energizing his body and the work of the body members among themselves are spiritual and miraculous in nature since they are energized by Christ and the Spirit. In this sense, the church should not be considered fundamentally as an organization but rather as a spiritual organism.

THE MANIFESTATION OF THE CHURCH: *UNIVERSAL AND LOCAL*

"The body of Christ" is a phrase that encompasses what is sometimes called the universal church. This refers to every individual believer in Christ, irrespective of land, language, denomination, or century in which they lived. All the believers of every nation, from the time the body of Christ was first formed at Pentecost (Acts 2:1-4) until the rapture, when the church will be taken to be with Christ (John 14:2-3; 17:24; 1 Cor 15:51-52; 1 Thess 4:13-18), make up the universal church.

One way the universal church manifests itself is through the gathering of its members in local assemblies or congregations geographically (e.g., Rom 1:7; 1 Cor 1:2; 2 Cor 1:1; Phil 1:1). In contrast to the universal body of Christ, these local gatherings may include individuals in attendance who are not part of the universal church, that is, they have not genuinely come to faith in Christ and therefore have not experienced salvation and are not part of the body of Christ.

THE BIRTH OF THE CHURCH

Although the plan for the church existed eternally, before time, in the mind and purpose of God, Jesus first announced that he would build his church in Matt 16:17-19. Speaking to Peter, he made known his plan,

> And Jesus said to him, "Blessed are you, Simon Barjona, because flesh and blood did not reveal *this* to you, but My Father who is in heaven. I also say to you that you are Peter, and upon this rock I will build My church; and the gates of Hades will not overpower it. I will give you the

> keys of the kingdom of heaven; and whatever you bind on earth shall have been bound in heaven, and whatever you loose on earth shall have been loosed in heaven."

What is significant for our discussion is the fact that the beginning of the church was designated as future when Christ said, "I *will* build My church" (emphasis added). This means the church was not yet in existence and would soon come into being as a new work of God. I pointed out earlier that the word ἐκκλησία (church) simply means gathering or assembly. It was used in the Greek translation of the Old Testament to describe the congregation of Israel, and Luke used the term to refer to a primarily Gentile crowd that had gathered in a theater in Ephesus (Deut 4:10; 9:10; 18:16; Acts 19:32). But when we come to the use of the term by Jesus, it takes on a more technical sense as we saw in Matt 16:18. Jesus prophesied that he would build his church. It was something that did not yet exist. Two chapters later, Jesus instructed the church how to practice discipline (Matt 18:17). But the actual birth of the church did not take place until after the death and resurrection of the Messiah. Luke mentioned the church as already existing in Acts 5:11, where he referred to a gathering of disciples or followers of Christ, "And great fear came over the whole *church*, and over all who heard of these things" (emphasis mine). We can conclude that the church began sometime after Christ had predicted its creation in Matt 16 but before Acts 5:11, where it is already in existence. There are good reasons to believe that it was birthed in Acts 2 when Jesus sent the Holy Spirit into the world, as he had promised he would do after his glorification, that is, after his death, resurrection, and ascension (John 7:38-39; 14:16-17, 26; 15:26; 16:7-15). Acts 2:1-4 record the event of the Holy Spirit being sent from heaven. In fact, Peter interpreted that event by saying, "Therefore having been exalted to the right hand of God, and having received from the Father the promise of the Holy Spirit, He has poured forth this which you both see and hear" (Acts 2:33). They saw a manifestation of the Spirit in the tongues of fire which were resting upon some of those present and they heard it through their speaking in tongues, that is, in foreign languages that were supernaturally given to those particular disciples (Acts 2:1-13).

What makes Jesus' church distinct from the gathering of Israelites in the Old Testament or even the secular gathering in Acts 19 is the miraculous work of the Holy Spirit in giving birth to this new entity, which the Apostle Paul called the body of Christ, in which Jews and Gentiles were united (1 Cor 12:13).

Historically, from that point on, each new believer becomes a member of the universal body of Christ, the church. Each member of the body of Christ is indwelt by the Father, the Son and the Holy Spirit (John 14:17, 23) and is spiritually gifted to glorify God and serve the body (Rom 12:3-8; 1 Cor 12; 1 Pet 4:10). Moreover, each believer is designated as a priest to God offering up to him spiritual service (Heb 13:15;1 Pet 2:5, 9).

This new spiritual priesthood is drawn not just from the nation of Israel but from all nations of the world (Matt 28:19-20; Rev 5:9). Once the church began, the nation of Israel did not cease to exist. Throughout the book of Acts, the church and the nation of Israel existed side by side. Israel always referred to the nation made up of ethnic Jews, and the church always referred to a gathering of Christ followers, whether Jew or Gentile. Luke did not confuse or conflate those two entities.

PART II

The Purpose(s) OF THE CHURCH ON EARTH

To this point, I have mainly attempted to bring together some of the major theological truths regarding Christ and his church. The church had its divine beginning in the mind of God in eternity past and was brought into being on earth with the pouring out of the Spirit at Pentecost (Acts 2:1-4). The Apostle John makes clear that the church has a heavenly destination and that Christ desires for it to be with him in heaven,

> In My Father's house are many dwelling places; if it were not so, I would have told you; for I go to prepare a place for you. If I go and prepare a place for you, I will come again and receive you to Myself, that where I am, there you may be also (John 14:2-3).

> Father, I desire that they also, whom You have given Me, be with Me where I am, so that they may see My glory which You have given Me, for You loved Me before the foundation of the world (John 17:24).

If Christ desires the church to be with him, why then has he left it in the world? The answer to that question is that the church has been tasked with specific purposes to fulfill during its earthly sojourn, before Christ takes it to be with himself. Much has been written about those purposes. I only intend to reiterate, briefly, three of its main tasks.

THE GREAT COMMISSION

Perhaps the most obvious and most often cited assignment given to the church is what we call the Great Commission. This commission is found in the three Synoptic Gospels, but most famously in Matthew:

> And Jesus came up and spoke to them, saying, "All authority has been given to Me in heaven and on earth. Go therefore and make disciples of all the nations, baptizing them in the name of the Father and the Son and the Holy Spirit, teaching them to observe all that I commanded you; and lo, I am with you always, even to the end of the age" (Matt 28:18-20).

Several observations are in order. This command is backed by the authority of Christ: "All authority has been given to me in heaven and on earth." The command is valid and in effect "even to the end of the age," which alludes to the second coming of Christ. The core command and main verb is to "make disciples" of all the nations. This means at least two things. The gospel message is to be taken and preached to the peoples and individuals of every nation of the earth. The term for nation refers most likely not just to those individual nations that we observe today but also to every people group (ethnos) within each nation. Many, if not most, nations have several people groups within their borders. Second, those who come to faith are to be baptized, publicly demonstrating their conversion to Christ. Third, the commission does not just involve evangelism and baptism of new believers, but also the training of those new believers to become devoted followers of Christ, that is, "disciples." This task is accomplished in part by "Teaching them to observe all that I commanded." The idea of observing is to obey and carry out the teaching of Christ. This task of making disciples has not yet been completed but rather is ongoing and will not be fulfilled before Christ comes to take his church home. The power and guidance for the commission is expressed in the words, "Lo, I am with you always, even to the end of the age." Christ is the one who calls and empowers his church to carry out this task. In the case of the Apostle Paul, Christ first called him to faith, and the Holy Spirit subsequently called him to the work of taking the gospel into Asia Minor (Acts 9:3-19; 13:1-3).

The Great Commission involves both evangelism and discipleship, at home and in the missionary enterprise of taking the gospel and making disciples of all nations, that is, of all people groups in the world. Any local church that is not taking part in this commission, both at home and abroad, is not fulfilling one of the essential purposes for its existence. Although the Great Commission is one of the main purposes for the existence of the church on earth, it is by no means its only purpose. Before we look at two other purposes, it should be pointed out that the Great Commission is the only purpose that can take place here on earth and not in heaven, and it is for that reason of paramount importance.

Some mission organizations maintain that social work should be considered as one of the distinct purposes of the church. Practitioners who hold this view argue that it is part of the commission of "teaching them to observe all that I commanded you." Social work, such as building hospitals and schools, offering medical aid, feeding the hungry, caring for the poor, teaching farming, etc., is indeed good and helpful, and in some cases even necessary in aiding the missionary in his or her task of making disciples. However, such works do not comprise the main commission as spelled out in Matt 28:19-20 and should not supplant the work of disseminating the gospel and making disciples. Christ did not specifically commission the church to engage in social work in the same way that he commanded it to take the gospel to all nations. Therefore, it seems better to view social work (and other forms of good works) not as the main commission itself but rather means through which the commission can be fulfilled. They aid mission agencies and individuals in gaining access to peoples and nations for the purpose of showing love and ultimately sharing the gospel and making disciples.

EDIFICATION OF THE SAINTS

A second purpose for the church's earthly existence is what is sometimes called the edification of the saints, or the building up of itself in love (Eph 4:11-16). This is the divinely intended means of facilitating spiritual growth necessary for caring for its members and for training them in ministry. The edification of the church also contributes to its ability to carry out two of its other purposes, namely the Great Commission and the worship of God in spirit and truth.

Although Christ reigns supreme as head over the church, he has also appointed human leaders as under-shepherds to nurture the body of Christ. The apostles appointed spiritual leaders in the local churches and designated them as elders, bishops, or pastors who normally served in a plurality (Acts 14:23; 20:17, 28; Phil 1:1; 1 Tim 3:1-7). In addition, deacons were appointed as servants in the churches. Whereas elders concerned themselves primarily with spiritual ministries, the deacons were more focused on practical service (Phil 1:1; 1 Tim 3:8-10, 12-13). God gave these leaders and other gifted individuals to the church for the express purpose of training the body of Christ to do the work of ministry:

> And He gave some *as* apostles, and some *as* prophets, and some *as* evangelists, and some as pastors and teachers, for the equipping of the saints for the work of service, to the building up of the body of Christ (Eph 4:11-12).

This particular function of gifted church leaders is to continue until the body of Christ reaches spiritual maturity:

> until we all attain to the unity of the faith, and of the knowledge of the Son of God, to a mature man, to the measure of the stature which belongs to the fullness of Christ (Eph 4:13).

The ministry of these gifted leaders was also to protect the church from false teachers and false teaching:

> As a result, we are no longer to be children, tossed here and there by waves and carried about by every wind of doctrine, by the trickery of men, by craftiness in deceitful scheming (Eph 4:14).

In addition to providing gifted leaders for the church, Christ, the head of the Church, has also granted to each member of his body a spiritual gift or gifts, which are Spirit-energized capacities for glorifying God and edifying other believers. At the point of salvation, when the Holy Spirit takes up residence in the believer, He sovereignly grants these spiritual capacities or gifts to each believer. The New Testament passages that reveal the gifts are Rom 12:3-8; 1 Cor 12-14; Eph 4:7-13; and 1 Pet 4:10-11.

I am often puzzled by churches that enthusiastically support the Matt 28:18-20 command, yet greatly undervalue this purpose of building up the body of Christ. They view the purpose of Sunday morning or, in some cases, mid-week worship services as having primarily an evangelistic aim rather than as a training ground for the edification of believers. This dereliction is usually most telling in the lack of depth in preaching that we hear in some churches on Sunday mornings. It is praiseworthy that the gospel is given out and men and women are called to faith in Christ, but it is lamentable when that happens to the neglect of feeding the body of Christ the word of God. The one should be done without failing to do the other.

A question we must pose is this: according to New Testament revelation, for whom was the weekly or regular gathering of the saints designed? Was it designed by God to be primarily evangelistic, or was it designed by God to function primarily as a gathering in which the body of Christ would be built up in its faith? Of course, the weekly gathering is to serve both of these purposes, but the question here is which is primary? Where should the emphasis lie? In Acts and the epistles, we can observe that believers came together on the first day of the week (Acts 20:7; 1 Cor 16:2). The writer of Hebrews commands us that we should not forsake the gathering of ourselves together (Heb 10:24). My point here is not to argue that Sundays are the only day on which we can assemble. We can assemble any day of the week, as the Apostle Paul makes clear (Rom 14:5-6). But after the resurrection of Christ on the first day of the week, believers began to gather overwhelmingly on Sundays. Was the purpose of such gatherings primarily evangelistic? Unbelievers did visit the early churches. For example, Paul writes to the Corinthians,

> Therefore if the whole church assembles together and all speak in tongues, and ungifted men or unbelievers enter, will they not say that you are mad? (1 Cor 14:23).

Clearly, he expected some unbelievers to visit the church at Corinth. But was the primary purpose of the gathering for unbelievers who might visit the church or for the believers to worship and be built up in their faith? Were the services designed for the non-believing world or for the believers? Preaching the gospel to the non-believer is one of the purposes for the existence of the church, but the main purpose for the regular gathering of the saints was for building up and edifying the believers so that they are equipped to worship and serve God, minister to other believers, and share the gospel with their contemporaries outside of the formal church gatherings.

I remember several years ago talking to a friend, who lamented to me that his first seventeen years in church were really just one year. I asked him what he meant. He said he sat in the church each Sunday morning for seventeen years, but it was as though he had sat through the first year seventeen times. He complained that the preaching was directed primarily at non-believers and seekers, not at believers. He was lamenting the fact that he did not grow much in his faith during those years.

The purpose for the gathering of the church, apart from worship, is for the edification of the believers. It is to feed the flock. We see in Acts 2:42 the basic components of the early weekly gatherings:

> They were continually devoting themselves to the apostles' teaching and to fellowship, to the breaking of bread and to prayer.

Evangelism is conspicuously absent from that list. This is not to say the gospel should not be given out in the Sunday morning gathering; it should and must. But evangelism is not the primary purpose of the meeting; edification of the saints is. This means the content of worship and teaching is to be primarily directed toward the worship of God, feeding the sheep, and edifying the body. When we focus on training and edifying the body with the Word of God, we enable and equip believers to do the work of ministry. The body of believers is to ministers to itself through healing, encouraging, strengthening, and training itself to do the work of ministry. This important purpose of edification is expressed in the following passage:

> but speaking the truth in love, we are to grow up in all *aspects* into Him who is the head, *even* Christ, from whom the whole body, being fitted and held together by what every joint supplies, according to the proper working of each individual part, causes the growth of the body for the building up of itself in love (Eph 4:15-16).

This ministry function of the body is, of course, not limited to a Sunday morning gathering. Through the fellowship of the body, by the exercise of the spiritual gifts of its members, mutual edification and training take place whenever believers gather. We see in the above passage that every member is part of the body and contributes to its growth so that all are built up in our faith. The idea of an individual believer in Christ not participating in a local gathering is foreign to the New Testament. Each believer is needed by other believers, and every saint needs the nurture provided by other saints. Without this mutual interaction between believers, the spiritual growth of the individual follower of Christ will be stunted.

The goal of building up the body of Christ is to bring every believer to maturity. To accomplish this goal, members of the body of Christ need one another. This becomes readily apparent by observing the "one-another" concepts in the New Testament. Well over fifty times the phrase is used to refer to the mutual edification that is to take place in the local gatherings. By way of summary, these include but are not limited to,

> *loving one another, being devoted to one another, having the same mind as one another, not judging one another hypocritically, building up one another; accepting, admonishing, greeting, caring for, and serving one another, not challenging, not*

> *envying or devouring one another, not lying to one another, being kind to one another, submitting, comforting, seeking one another's good, encouraging one another, not speaking or complaining against one another, being hospitable to, showing humility to, and having fellowship with one another, and teaching one another.*

The multiple one-another concepts demonstrate the importance and focus in the gatherings of the local churches. This profuse in-depth interaction of believers with each other is designed for the spiritual welfare of each believer, not just what one can receive but also what each one can offer to another believer. Though attending church gatherings may not be the natural tendency of some of us, it is nevertheless God's prescription for our growth. Failure to pursue or engage in this fellowship not only hinders our growth but also the growth of others. Since the one-another concepts are imperatives, a refusal to participate in the body-life of a local church sadly falls into the category of disobedience.

One major aspect of the regular edification of believers in the local churches must be the weekly teaching or preaching of the Word of God. When Paul appointed his protégé Timothy to pastor the church at Ephesus, he gave him this command,

> I solemnly charge *you* in the presence of God and of Christ Jesus, who is to judge the living and the dead, and by His appearing and His kingdom: preach the word; be ready in season *and* out of season; reprove, rebuke, exhort, with great patience and instruction (2 Tim 4:1-2).

The importance of teaching is also seen in the following commands that Paul gave Timothy,

> Prescribe and teach these things (1 Tim 4:11).

> Teach and preach these *principles* (1 Tim 6:2).

> The things which you have heard from me…entrust these to faithful men who will be able to teach others also (2 Tim 2:2).

> The Lord's bondservant must…be…able to teach (2 Tim 2:24).

The goal of the saints gathering is clearly expressed by Paul in his letter to the Colossians,

> We proclaim Him, admonishing every man and teaching every man with all wisdom, so that we may present every man complete in Christ (Col 1:28).

Bringing every man and woman to maturity in Christ means helping them to grow in their faith and become more like Christ in their character,

> For those whom He foreknew, He also predestined *to become* conformed to the image of His Son, so that He would be the firstborn among many brethren (Rom 8:29).

> But we all, with unveiled face, beholding as in a mirror the glory of the Lord, are being transformed into the same image from glory to glory, just as from the Lord, the Spirit (2 Cor 3:18).

God promises to work towards this goal until the church's sojourn on earth is complete,

> *For I am* confident of this very thing, that He who began a good work in you will perfect it until the day of Christ Jesus (Phil 1:6).

A by-product of this gathering of the saints and the organic function of the body is that non-believers are drawn to Christ through it, and thus, even in this way, the Great Commission is being served.

> "By this all men will know that you are My disciples, if you have love for one another" (John 13:35).

> "I in them and You in Me, that they may be perfected in unity, so that the world may know that You sent Me, and loved them, even as You have loved Me" (John 17:23).

In this way the church functions as a light to the world, drawing people towards Christ with the hope of them coming to faith in him,

> "You are the light of the world. A city set on a hill cannot be hidden; nor does *anyone* light a lamp and put it under a basket, but on the lampstand, and it gives light to all who are in the house. Let your light shine before men in such a way that they may see your good works, and glorify your Father who is in heaven" (Matt 5:14-16).

Paul makes clear that one of our Lord's objectives with his church is for it to serve the world through its good works and, in so doing, draw men and women to Christ.

> For we are His workmanship, created in Christ Jesus for good works, which God prepared beforehand so that we would walk in them (Eph 2:10).

Thus, the edification of believers is one of the main purposes of the church in its temporary earthly sojourn. It not only strengthens the church, but it also is one of the means by which the church carries out its evangelistic mission.

THE WORSHIP OF GOD

It goes without saying that a major purpose of the church is the worship of God. This is the most fundamental and essential of the purposes of Christ's church. We were redeemed for a purpose. In fact, we can unreservedly say that the ultimate goal of the great commission and the strengthening of the church is to make true worshipers of God.

> "But an hour is coming, and now is, when the true worshipers will worship the Father in spirit and truth; for such people the Father seeks to be His worshipers. God is spirit, and those who worship Him must worship in spirit and truth" (John 4:23-24).

God is on a quest to make true worshipers. No man or woman can become a true worshiper of God without first being born again or born from above (John 3:3). Thus, the Great Commission serves the ultimate purpose of making new worshipers of God. In his defense before King Agrippa, the Apostle Paul proclaimed that God had called and appointed him to be a witness to both the Jews and the Gentiles for this express purpose:

> to open their eyes so that they may turn from darkness to light and from the dominion of Satan to God (Acts 26:18).

Satan has "blinded the minds of the unbelieving" so that they cannot and will not recognize and believe in God's Savior (2 Cor 4:4). It is for this reason that God must seek out the lost to deliver them judgment and transform them into God worshipers.

In heaven, worship is grounded upon two divine truths. The first is that God is the creator of all things:

> Worthy are You, our Lord and our God, to receive glory and honor and power; for You created all things, and because of Your will they existed, and were created (Rev 4:11).

The second ground for worship is that Jesus, the Lamb of God, provided redemption through his blood:

> And they sang a new song, saying, worthy are You to take the book and to break its seals; for You were slain, and purchased for God with Your blood *men* from every tribe and tongue and people and nation (Rev 5:9-10).

The more new worshipers of God are built up in their faith, the more they are enabled to worship God "in spirit and truth" (John 4:23-25). So, we see that the first two purposes of the church, which I addressed above (evangelism and edification), serve the ultimate purpose of worshiping and serving God.

God has given us great freedom to creatively fulfill these major purposes of evangelism and discipleship, edification of the body of Christ, and the worship of God. Other ancillary purposes for the church could be cited, but these appear to be the major tasks that God has given to his church in its earthly sojourn.

THE CHURCH'S STRUGGLE IN A HOSTILE WORLD

Although Christ desires the church to be with him and to experience his glory, it is not God's purpose to remove it from the world until the end of the age (John 14:2-3; 17:15, 24; 1 Thess 4:13-18; 1 John 3:2). He left the church on earth to complete the purposes iterated above. In the world the church finds itself in a hostile environment. The great conflict between good and evil began with the fall of Satan and the host of rebellious angels that followed him (Isa 14:12; Ezek 28:12-17; Matt 25:41; Rev 12:4). That conflict was brought to earth in Gen 3. Since the fall of man in the Garden, the world has largely remained hostile territory for God and his purposes. Though God remains the ultimate Sovereign, Satan has claimed control of the earth and has even been acknowledged as the "god of this world" (Luke 4:6; John 12:31; 2 Cor 4:4). He directs his hostility not only at God but also at God's people, at Israel since the nation was founded and at the church since it was formed. Numerous demonic principalities (fallen angels) from the spiritual realm work with him to frustrate God's purposes. These powers then manifest their malevolence by using human instruments. Let me cite two examples of this spiritual conflict in the Old Testament.

In 2 Kgs 6, the Aramean army surrounded the city of Dothan, where God's prophet, Elisha, and his attendant were held up. The attendant was frightened when he saw the army. Elisha prayed that God would open the eyes of his attendant to see the spiritual nature of the battle. God answered that prayer, and in 2 Kgs 6:17 the inspired writer tells us the following:

> And the Lord opened the servant's eyes and he saw; and behold, the mountain was full of horses and chariots of fire all around Elisha.

What Elisha's attendant saw were spiritual forces protecting Elisha from the physical forces arrayed against him. That story provides us with a view of the reality of spiritual warfare.

Another example is found in Dan 10. Daniel received a message in the form of a vision from God that was "true and one of great conflict" (Dan 10:1). Daniel had been praying for his nation for three weeks. As a response to his prayer, a glorious angel appeared to him and explained that he had been trying to come to Daniel from the time that the prophet had begun to pray but had been hindered by the "prince of the Kingdom of Persia." That prince was apparently a demonic angel who was attempting to influence the Persian empire in its treatment of the Jews. The angel told Daniel that Michael (the Archangel) came to help him in the fight against that demonic prince, thus freeing him up to come to Daniel with God's message. After the vision and message were given, the angel told Daniel he must leave the prophet to continue in his struggle against the evil forces of the Persian empire and those that will afterwards in the Greek empire. That revelation pulls back the curtain of the spiritual realm and allows us to see the warfare that was taking place in the angelic world. It was one of hostility towards God's good purposes and plans for his people.

However, the greatest hostility that was ever mounted against God is revealed to us in the Gospels, in the brutal murder of the Messiah. Satan entered into Judas, using him in the plot to kill Jesus (Luke 22:3-5). Jesus interprets the event as one energized by "the power of darkness" (Luke 22:53). What does all this have to do with the church? Jesus warned his followers that they should expect to experience the same hostility that he did,

> "If the world hates you, you know that it has hated Me before it hated You" (John 15:18).

> "an hour is coming for everyone who kills you to think that he is offering service to God. These things they will do because they have not known the Father or Me. But these things I have spoken to you, so that when their hour comes, you may remember that I told you of them. These things I did not say to you at the beginning, because I was with you" (John 16:2-4).

In more recent times, the church in the Western world has enjoyed a measure of freedom and peace, yet the general tenor of church history has been one of persecution, brutality, and hatred directed towards God's people from the world. In the present hour, the church throughout the world faces varying degrees of persecution from its respective governments. Yet, Jesus has intentionally left the church in the world as a testimony to the reality of God's saving purposes (Matt 5:14-16; John 17:15-16). We should not anticipate that the world will ever embrace us but rather that we will face an ongoing struggle.

> "Remember the word that I said to you: A servant is not greater than his master. If they persecuted me, they will

> also persecute you. If they kept my word, they will also keep yours" (John 15:20).
>
> Do not be surprised, brethren, if the world hates you (1 John 3:13)

Although some forms of Christianity, post-millennialism and Christian Nationalism, for example, believe that the church will experience a gradual increase of influence in the world, history and Scripture seem to indicate otherwise (Phil 3:20).

The Apostle Paul unveils the reality of the church's spiritual struggle in his letter to the Ephesians:

> For our struggle is not against flesh and blood, but against the rulers, against the powers, against the world forces of this darkness, against the spiritual forces of wickedness in the heavenly places (Eph 6:12).

It is in the context of this spiritual conflict that Paul calls the church to prayer "at all times in the spirit" (Eph 6:18). This struggle is manifested not only in the physical realm through persecution and hatred but also in the inward battle of ideas, where scriptural truth collides with human philosophy.

> For though we walk in the flesh, we do not war according to the flesh, for the weapons of our warfare are not of the flesh, but divinely powerful for the destruction of fortresses. We are destroying speculations and every lofty thing raised up against the knowledge of God, and we are taking every thought captive to the obedience of Christ (2 Cor 10:3-5).

Through the preaching and teaching of the word of God, the church is to engage in refuting false doctrine and false ideas about God (2 Tim 4:1-5; Titus 1:9; 2:1).

It is in the context of this earthly and spiritual struggle that the church is called to engage in the three great purposes delineated above: the Great Commission, building itself up in love, and worshiping the one true God.

THE CHURCH'S MANIFESTATION TO THE SPIRITUAL WORLD

We have briefly explored three of the main functions the church is to have on earth. The church also serves a heavenly-directed purpose during its time on earth. Paul explains this in Eph 3:10,

> so that the manifold wisdom of God might now be made known through the church to the rulers and the authorities in the heavenly *places*.

The wisdom of God is being manifested through the church "to the rulers and authorities in the heavenly places," that is, to the angels. Paul explains that the particular wisdom communicated by the church concerns the inclusion of Gentiles as coheirs in the body of Christ (Eph 3:6). This truth can be observed by angels whenever and wherever a person, Gentile or Jew, becomes part of the body of Christ. Apparently, God is using the Jew-Gentile unity of the body of Christ as an object lesson directed at angels (perhaps both good and fallen) by demonstrating his character and work of mercy and grace in calling and perfecting the church.

Other Scriptures confirm that angelic beings observe the church. For example, the apostles had become a spectacle "to angels" (1 Cor 4:9), and when Paul charged Timothy, he did so in the presence of the "chosen angels" (1 Tim 5:21). The writer of Hebrews indicates that angels are ministering spirits who render service to all who will inherit salvation (Heb 1:14). The phenomenon of angels observing the church is also reflected in Paul's letter to the Corinthians where he writes that women were to have their heads covered "because of the angels." Apparently, angels observed the male-female creation order by the women covering their heads—ostensibly with hair since that is the only covering specifically mentioned in the passage (1 Cor 11:10, 15). This is all to say that the church serves as an object lesson of certain spiritual truths to the angels.

PART III

The Church

AND THE MYSTERIES OF THE KINGDOM

The church is one part or feature of God's kingdom program, but the two are not exactly synonymous, for the kingdom is much more expansive. For example, the kingdom of God can refer to God's sovereign eternal rule over the entire universe—nothing excluded, "The LORD has established His throne in the heavens, and His sovereignty rules over all" (Ps 103:19). The writer of Chronicles says it this way, "Yours, O Lord, is the greatness and the power and the glory and the victory and the majesty, indeed everything that is in the heavens and the earth; Yours is the dominion, O Lord, and You exalt Yourself as head over all" (1 Chron 29:11). Notice that in the Chronicles passage the writer states that the LORD has dominion over "everything" in heaven and earth, this includes the non-believing world. The prophet Daniel succinctly states, "His dominion is an everlasting dominion, and His kingdom *endures* from generation to generation" (cf. Ps 145:13; Dan 4:3, 34). This all-encompassing idea of the kingdom includes all things and all events. Both good and evil are under his rule, "The One forming light and creating darkness, causing well-being and creating calamity; I am the LORD who does all these" (Isa 45:7). This does not mean that God is the author of evil, for "God is light and in Him there is no darkness at all" (1 John 1:5). But it does mean that evil is under his sovereign rule. The prophet Amos states it this way, "If a trumpet is blown in a city will not the people tremble? If a calamity occurs in a city has not the LORD done it?" (Amos 3:6). This concept of God's sovereign kingdom has no condition for entrance; all men and all things are part of it and under its rule, whether they know it or not.

By way of contrast, God's rulership in Israel in the Old Testament was a historical form of his rule that differed from his sovereign rule over all things. God did not rule over the Gentile nations in the same way he ruled over Israel. The manifestation of God's glory signaled his direct presence among the Israelites. He first began to dwell among them by means of his glory cloud during their wanderings in the wilderness (Exod 13:21-22). Once the tabernacle was erected, his glory took up residence in it (Exod 40:34-38). Later, at the time of Solomon, his glory filled the temple (1 Kgs 8:10-13). God's pledge in the Davidic Covenant was a promise of the continuation of this kingdom in Israel. God vowed that he would establish the throne and kingdom of one of David's descendants forever (2 Sam 7:1-14; 1 Chron 17:7-14; Ps 89:3-4, 20-29). That form of the kingdom in Israel was temporarily terminated at the Babylonian captivity when God's glory departed from the temple (Ezek 8:1-4; 10:3-5, 18-19; 11:22-23). Later, when the New Testament opens, Luke tells us that Jesus was the one who would reestablish the kingdom promised to David. Referring to Jesus, Luke writes,

> He will be great and will be called the Son of the Most High; and the Lord God will give Him the throne of His father David; and He will reign over the house of

> Jacob forever, and His kingdom will have no end (Luke 1:32-33).

It is worth noting that when Jesus began his ministry, he stated that the kingdom was "at hand." But there were certain conditions for entrance to the kingdom, namely repentance (Matt 4:17; Luke 17:21). Not everyone and everything was part of that kingdom, nor were the Israelites unless they repented. So, it seems clear that the kingdom in Israel was not the same as God's eternal kingdom involving his rule over everything.

The mystery kingdom that encompasses our present age is another manifestation of God's kingdom rule (Mark 4:11), which I will describe shortly in greater detail. It is not the same as God's sovereign rule over all things, nor is it the same as His rule in Israel during much of the nation's history, nor should it be equated with the future kingdom that is coming to earth, "Your kingdom come, your will be done on earth as it is in heaven" (Matt 6:10). The fact that the kingdom mentioned in Matt 6:10 still needs to "come" makes clear that it is not the same as God's universal sovereign rule over all things, for that universal kingdom has always existed, nor can it be equated with the kingdom that now exists in the church, for that manifestation of the kingdom is already present, but rather it refers to a future manifestation of God's rule over Israel and indeed over the whole earth. In the book of Revelation, the Apostle John identifies this future kingdom as about to arrive,

> The kingdom of the world has become *the kingdom* of our Lord and of His Christ; and He will reign forever and ever...Now the salvation, and the power, and the kingdom of our God and the authority of His Christ have come...(Rev 11:15; 12:10).

In Rev 20, John more specifically identifies that kingdom as a thousand year reign, a rule confirmed by many Old and New Testament Scriptures (cf. Ps 72:8-17; Isa 9:6-7; 11:1-10; 24:23; 65:20-25; Ezek 40–48; Mic 4:7; Zech 14:9; Matt 6:10; 19:27-28; Luke 1:33; Acts 1:6; Rev 11:15; 12:10; 20:1-8). My point in this brief survey of God's kingdom is that there have been various manifestations of it in history.

In light of Israel's rejection of Jesus as their Messiah, our Lord begins to reveal what would happen to the kingdom that he had been announcing from the start of his ministry (Matt 4:17; Mark 1:14-15). In short, the Davidic kingdom promised in 2 Sam 7:1-14, referred to by the angel Gabriel before the Messiah was born (Luke 1:31-33) and announced at the start of Jesus' ministry, would be withdrawn or postponed due to the nation's rejection of the Messiah (Matt 21:43).

> Therefore I say to you, the kingdom of God will be taken away from you and given to a people, producing the fruit of it (Matt 21:43).

In the meantime, the kingdom work of God in the present age would take on a new form. In Matt 13:11, Mark 4:11, and Luke 8:10, Jesus employed the term "mysteries" (Mark refers to it in the singular as a "mystery") to refer to new revelations about the kingdom in the present age. These new truths about the mystery kingdom had not been taught in the Old Testament era but had now come to light. Matthew says they were "things hidden from the foundation of the world" (Matt 13:35). They were newly revealed because Israel had rejected Jesus, the Davidic king. They clarify what would happen in relation to the advancement of God's kingdom in the present age. The principal manifestation of the mystery kingdom in our current age is the church. Thus, the spread of the kingdom in this age is largely synonymous with the growth of the church.[4] Paul refers to the believer's salvation as entrance into this kingdom,

> For He rescued us from the domain of darkness, and transferred us to the kingdom of His beloved Son (Col 1:13).

THE MYSTERIES IN THE KINGDOM PARABLES

New truths about the kingdom of God in our present age were given by Jesus in the form of parables. The reason for this is that parables served the dual purpose of revealing new truth to those who were responding in faith to the Messiah (Matt 13:11-12, 16-17, 52) while at the same time hiding these same truths from those who were rejecting him (Matt 13:11b, 13-15). Hiding truth from those rejecting the Messiah was a form of judgment on their willful unbelief and rejection (Isa 6:10; Matt 13:14-15).

The kingdom parables chronicle the spiritual progress of God's kingdom in the present age. For that reason, they apply to the Church. These parables begin with the propagation of the kingdom message (the parable of the sower) and end with the second coming of the Messiah to earth and the establishment of his kingdom (the parable of the dragnet). Matthew 13:52 reveals that these parables teach both old and new truths,

> Therefore, every scribe who has become a disciple of the kingdom of heaven is like a head of a household, who brings out of his treasure things new and old.

This means that these parables contain old truths carried over from the Old Testament revelation about the kingdom and new

---

4 One notable difference between the mystery kingdom in the present age and the church as a mystery form of the kingdom; this is depicted in the parable of the sower which began with the dissemination of the kingdom message (not the gospel) during Jesus' earthly ministry. By way of contrast, the church did not begin until after the Messiah's death, resurrection, ascension, and sending of the Holy Spirit (cf. Matt 16:18; John 7:39; 14:16-17, 26; Acts 2:1-4). Another contrast is that the church continues on earth up to the time of its rapture or translation from the earth (John 14:2-3; 1 Cor 15: 50-54; 1 Thess 4:13-17), but the mystery form of the kingdom lasts until the second coming of Christ to earth in judgment (Matt 13:30, 40-43, 49-50).

truths that were not revealed in the Old Testament. These new truths are now brought to light in view of Israel's rejection of her Messiah. The parables in question are most extensively revealed in Matt 13 but also in Mark 4 and in Luke 8:4-18; 13:18-21.

The term "mysteries" was employed by Jesus in Matt 13:11 to describe these truths about the kingdom,

> Jesus answered them, "To you it has been granted to know the mysteries of the kingdom of heaven, but to them it has not been granted.

By way of comparison, Mark, recording the same parables, writes,

> And He was saying to them, "To you has been given the mystery of the kingdom of God, but those who are outside get everything in parables" (Mark 4:11).

In other words, Jesus was withholding insight into the mystery from those who were rejecting him but giving understanding to those who were his genuine followers. Because there is an overlap between the kingdom in this age and the church, it is helpful to observe what the following parables teach about the kingdom so we can also observe what they depict about the growth of the church.

1. *The Parable of the Sower* (Matt 13:3-9, 18-23).

In this parable a sower distributes seed that falls on various soils. The seed is the "word of the kingdom," not the message about the death and resurrection of the Messiah. The soils produce various results illustrating the differing responses to the kingdom message (13:1-9, 18-23). The view of the coming kingdom in the Old Testament was that God would suddenly intervene with great power to establish it on the earth and the Jews felt they would all automatically be part of it since they were descendants of Abraham (cf. Dan 2:44; 7:27; Luke 3:8; John 8:33). But the parable of the sower revealed that the message of the Messiah's kingdom, the "seed" sown, would not be accepted by the majority of those who heard it, in fact it would be rejected by most, for various reasons. This new reality was not foreseen in the Old Testament's view of the coming messianic kingdom, but was now part of the kingdom truth in the current age.

Although the church is not specifically mentioned in this parable, nor in the rest of the parables of this chapter, it nevertheless shares a history with these kingdom truths. The message of the church in this present age is not the message of the promised Davidic kingdom, but rather the gospel. This is the message that Christ has died for our sins and that faith in Him and in what he did for us on the cross provides forgiveness of sins. As depicted in the parable of the sower, the majority of people who heard the message of the kingdom did not respond in faith to it. The same can be said about the message of the gospel. Most do not respond in faith but have rejected it for the same reasons that the parable cites, but the good news is that some do believe. These are depicted as "the good soil" (Matt 13:8, 23). This parable helps the church understand how the world responds to the gospel.

2. *The Parable of the Growing Seed* (Mark 4:26-29).

In this parable (found only in Mark) a man cast seed upon the soil, and it grows while the man is sleeping. When he rises from his rest, he observes that the seed has sprouted and is growing. The parable teaches that in this age the kingdom would mysteriously grow, but the nature and power of that growth would not be visible to the human eye (depicted by the man sleeping). The fact that the growth takes place while the man sleeps indicates that the growth cannot be attributed to mere human effort but rather to the invisible supernatural work of God. What was new in this teaching was that the kingdom in the present age would not come suddenly with dramatic visible power as portrayed by the Old Testament prophets, but rather by an invisible spiritual power, and its spread would involve a gradual process akin to the growth of a plant. We can observe this growth of the church in the book of Acts. After the death and resurrection of the Messiah, the Spirit began to miraculously draw men and women to faith upon hearing the gospel message (John 16:7-11; Acts 2:41; 4:4; 10:42-44; 16:14). The growth was not caused by mere human effort but rather, as the Apostle Paul noted, it was the work of God, "So then neither the one who plants nor the one who waters is anything, but God who causes the growth" (1 Cor 3:7). The book of Acts reveals that it was the sovereign work of God that directed the dissemination of and response to the gospel message (Acts 2:1-4; 8:14-17, 26; 9:6, 15; 10:44-45; 13:2-4; 16:6-10, etc.). Though God uses human instruments to advance the gospel, the effective salvific work is carried out by the Spirit and thus invisible to the human eye. The parable ends with the plant reaching maturity and being harvested. Thus, the growth of the church will at some point reach completion. Paul refers to this maturity as "the fullness of the Gentiles" (Rom 11:25) when God will take the church to be with himself (John 14:2-3; 1 Cor 15:52; 1 Thess 4:16-17).

3. *The Parable of the Wheat and Tares* (Matt 13:24-30, 36-43).

In this parable, good seed is sown, but an enemy sows bad seed alongside it. As the two seeds grow, the difference between them is indiscernible. The two grow together until the end of the age, when they are separated. The crop of tares produced by the bad seed will be separated for judgment, while the harvest generated by the good seed, the wheat, will be gathered into God's kingdom. The parable reveals Satan's work of opposing and imitating the message of the Messiah. It results in believers and non-believers (wheat and tares) coexisting in the present world. In this parable, the "field" is not identified as the church but rather the "world." In the present age it is not God's purpose to remove the church from the world but rather for it to remain on earth as a witness, "I do not ask You to take them out of the world, but to keep them from the evil one. They are not of the world, even as I am not of the world" (John 17:15-16). During this age the church remains in the world until God determines to remove it (1 Thess 4:13-18).

The newly revealed truth in the parable is the idea that in the present age both wheat and tares, believers and non-believers, co-exist and there would be a delay before the judgment of the wicked comes. "Allow both to grow together until the harvest and in the time of the harvest I will say to the reapers, 'First gather up the tares and bind them in bundles to burn them up; but gather the wheat into my barn'" (Matt 13:30).[5] The tares would not be removed until the second coming of Messiah in power and glory. Only then would the wheat enter into his kingdom symbolized by the word "barn." This concept is new because Israel expected that when her Messiah arrived, all opponents would be quickly eradicated. All unbelievers would be judged, and the kingdom would begin only with believers on the earth. That did not happen at Christ's First Coming because Israel had rejected her Messiah and his kingdom. But it will happen at the second coming.

4. *The Parable of the Mustard Seed* (Matt 13:31-32).

In this parable a tiny mustard seed is sown, but it eventually grows into a very large plant, so that even birds can nest in its branches. The parable reveals that in this present age the kingdom will start tiny in size. But there would be significant growth

5 For a possible distinction between the removal of the church from the earth and the gathering of the wheat into God's barn, one view is that that church is removed at the rapture which could occur at any time, but the wheat is gathered into the barn only after the Messiah's second coming to earth (see views on the rapture in the section titled: the end of the church's earthly sojourn).

over time. Its final size will contrast greatly with its beginning size. The birds nesting in its branches may imply that even those not directly part of the kingdom will nevertheless enjoy or take advantage of its influence, or it may mean that the kingdom will simply be a source of protection and rest for its participants. New was the concept that it would begin small and grow slowly, rather than suddenly engulf the whole earth as the Old Testament had portrayed (cf. Ps 72:8, 19; Isa 9:6-7; Dan 2:44; 7:27; Zech 9:10; 14:9). This new kingdom truth is reflected in the growth of the church in the book of Acts and throughout church history. The church began at Pentecost with a small group of Jews, the eleven disciples, and the 120 gathered in the upper room in Jerusalem (Acts 1:15; 2:1-4). It has continued to grow in numbers and spread geographically throughout church history. At times this growth has been explosive, as in the early chapters of Acts, and at other times almost unperceptively, and at other times in spurts.

5. *The Parable of the Leaven* (Matt 13:33).

In this parable the kingdom of God is compared to leaven hidden in a measure of flour. The leaven works invisibly and slowly to eventually leaven all the flour (the whole piece of dough). This parable may simply reveal that the kingdom in this age is invisible to the world. Its growth will be almost imperceptible yet continual until the whole world has been affected by it. The same could be said regarding the presence and growth of the church in the world. The new revelation would be that the kingdom will expand slowly in contrast to the Old Testament belief that it would break in upon the world suddenly with supernatural force (Ps 72:8, 19; Isa 9:6-7; Dan 2:44; 7:27; Zech 9:10; 14:9). In addition, this parable may signify something else. In the Bible, leaven always alludes to evil. If leaven symbolizes evil in this parable, then it is teaching that wickedness will continue to be present and spread in this age until the entire world is permeated by it. That was not expected in the kingdom projected by the Old Testament prophets.

6. *The Parable of the Hidden Treasure* (Matt 13:44).

In this parabolic comparison, Jesus says the kingdom of heaven is like a hidden treasure in a field which a man finds and re-hides. He then sells all his possessions to buy the field and obtain the treasure.[6] This is not teaching that a person must buy entrance to the kingdom. Rather, it is showing the priceless value of the kingdom and the joy it brings to the person who discovers or finds it. In contrast to the promised Davidic kingdom, its presence is not seen in an external glorious form, but rather it exists hidden from the human eye, hence the hidden treasure. But once it is found, or discovered, its value supersedes all earthly values. New is the idea that it is hidden or not readily visible and seemingly found by chance. How does this parable apply to God's work in the church? This parable could depict the person who was not necessarily seeking salvation but hears the gospel message, recognizes its phenomenal worth, and thus embraces Christ.

7. *The Parable of the Pearl of Great Price* (Matt 13:45).

In this parable, the kingdom is compared to a merchant seeking fine pearls. When he finds one of supreme value, he sells all he has to obtain it. This comparison is similar to the previous one, except in this case, the one obtaining the pearl searches diligently to find it, whereas the man who found the treasure in the field found it seemingly by chance. As in the previous parable, this one does not teach that the kingdom can be bought but

---

6 Some expositors suggest that in this parable and the following one the person buying the field and finding the pearl is the Messiah who valued the kingdom so much that he gave up his own life to purchase it. Though that theology is true, the focus in this series of parables seems to be the kingdom of God rather than the death of the Messiah.

that the kingdom itself is of such a supreme value that the one discovering it would gladly give up all wealth or earthly possessions to have it. New is the idea that the kingdom in this age is not externally observable as Old Testament saints expected it to be; it is hidden, and one needs to seek it in order to find it. How might this parable apply to God's work in the church? This parable could depict the person who is diligently seeking to find God, hears the gospel message, realizes its phenomenal worth, and thus embraces Christ.

8. *The Parable of the Dragnet* (Matt 13:47-50).

In this parable the kingdom of heaven in this age is compared to a dragnet that was cast into the sea and gathered both good and bad fish. Once the net was brought to shore, the bad fish were disposed of and the good fish kept. This parable revealed that the judgment of God will not separate the true and false believers until the end of the age; at that time, all the wicked will be judged, and the righteous will enter the kingdom (13:47-50). New is the idea that the kingdom in this age would consist of a mixture of believers and non-believers, and not until the end of the age would they be separated, and not until the consummation of the age would the Messiah establish his kingdom on earth. By way of contrast, the kingdom envisioned by the Old Testament prophets was to come suddenly from heaven with great power at the arrival of the Messiah. At that time the wicked were to be judged, and the good would be left to enter the kingdom. An intervening mystery form of the kingdom between the First and Second Advents had not been foreseen or envisioned.

9. *The Parable of the Householder* (Matt 13:52).

In this final parabolic comparison, Jesus says that a scribe who is a disciple of the kingdom is like the head of a household who has a treasure, and out of his treasure he brings both old and new things. This verse is key to understanding what Jesus is doing with these parables. He is teaching that the mystery form of the kingdom in this present age will have some features that are similar to the kingdom prophesied in the Old Testament, but other features that are entirely new.

All these parables reveal something about the advancement of God's kingdom in this age. The mystery form of the kingdom exhibits some characteristics similar to those taught in the Old Testament, but it also has some entirely new features that heretofore had not been revealed. The current form of the kingdom started small, but by the end of the age will be enormous. The spiritual power of God, which animates it, is invisible to the non-believing world. The age will continue with believers and non-believers living side by side in the world until the end. This current form of the kingdom and its growth are largely synonymous with the growth of the church.

By way of summary, in Matt 16:18, when Jesus prophesied that he would build his church, it was still future, "I will build My church." Acts 2 records the pouring out of the Spirit and the birth of the church. The following chapters in Acts chronicle its growth during its infancy. This was a new work of God that began at Pentecost and has continued throughout this age. The parables of Matt 13 characterize its growth. The church will not end its earthly sojourn until Christ comes to take her home to himself (cf. Acts 2:1-4; John 14:2-3; 1 Cor 15:50-55; 1 Thess 4:13-18).

PART IV

The End
OF THE CHURCH'S EARTHLY SOJOURN

APPROACHING THE END OF THE CHURCH AGE

People often ask or wonder if we are in the last days. The use of a phrase such as "later times" or its equivalent "the last days" must be viewed in its context because this kind of phrase refers to more than one time period. If people asking this question are referring to the technical sense that refers to the seventieth week of Daniel's prophecy or the apocalyptic judgments contained in the book of Revelation, then the answer would be no, we are not yet in the last days. But if they mean the last days in the more general sense as described by a few passages in the New Testament, we could affirm that we have been in the last days since the First Advent of the Messiah. A couple of passages refer to the last days as the period between the First and Second Advents. For example, Peter, in his message at Pentecost, says that the pouring out of the Spirit signaled that they were "in the last days" (Acts 2:17). Later, in one of his letters he confirms that it was "in the last times" that Jesus came as the Lamb of God providing redemption (1 Pet 1:20). The writer of Hebrews also affirms that he was already living in the last days when he wrote

"God…in these last days has spoken to us in His Son" (Heb 1:1-2). The Apostle John goes so far as to say he was living in the last hour, "Children, it is the last hour" (1 John 2:18). According to these Scriptures, the First Advent signaled the onset of the last days, which in those contexts refer to the church age in general but particularly as it nears its end. Even though we do not know the century, decade, year, month, week, day, or hour when the Lord will come to receive his church unto himself, we are given general characteristics of the time. A few NT passages describe the character of the later days of the church age as it nears its completion. In his first letter to Timothy, Paul writes,

> But the Spirit explicitly says that in later times some will fall away from the faith, paying attention to deceitful spirits and doctrines of demons (1 Tim 4:1).

Thus, as we near the end of the age, we can expect an increase in the teaching of false doctrine in churches, and many who once professed faith will abandon it. In his second letter to Timothy, Paul also describes the moral breakdown in the latter period of the church age:

> But realize this, that in the last days difficult times will come. For men will be lovers of self, lovers of money, boastful, arrogant, revilers, disobedient to parents, ungrateful, unholy, unloving, irreconcilable, malicious gossips, without self-control, brutal, haters of good, treacherous, reckless, conceited, lovers of pleasure rather than lovers of God, holding to a form of godliness, although they have denied its power; avoid such men as these (2 Tim 3:1-5).

The Apostle Peter also refers to this period of time,

> Know this first of all, that in the last days mockers will come with *their* mocking, following after their own lusts,

> and saying, "Where is the promise of His coming? For *ever* since the fathers fell asleep, all continues just as it was from the beginning of creation." (2 Pet 3:3-4).

False teachers and defectors from the faith have plagued the church from its beginning (Acts 20:29-31; 2 Pet 2:1-3; Jude 17-19), but they will increase as we draw near to the end of the age. Does this falling away from the faith in the latter days refer to genuine believers jettisoning their faith, or is it referring to the departure of many who are mere professors of faith in the Messiah? It will most likely be a combination of the two. However, it is important to note that if a genuine believer veers from the faith, like with other sins, God may give time for repentance or he may intervene with discipline leading to eventual restoration, or in some cases he may even take the believer home with an untimely death (cf. 1 Cor 11:30-32; Heb 12:5-8; 1 John 5:16; Rev 2:21). On the other hand, the apostacy of the last days will demonstrate that many who profess faith are not genuinely saved (Matt 13:25, 38; Heb 10:39). These apostates will pursue demonic doctrine. They have no love for God and deny the second coming of Christ. Some will have been leaders in the church but will eventually make a break with it,

> They went out from us, but they were not *really* of us; for if they had been of us, they would have remained with us; but *they went out*, so that it would be shown that they all are not of us (1 John 2:19).

What is important to realize is that as the church nears the end of its sojourn on earth, these characteristics of the last days will increase.

By way of summary, we have seen that the church, composed of the individual members of the body of Christ, has been chosen by God from all eternity. Each individual chosen is called to faith in Christ through the gospel during his or her lifetime. Through the new birth, each believer is spiritually united to Christ and his body (other believers). The corporate body of Christ manifests itself on earth in local assemblies. Since the birth of the church in Jerusalem at Pentecost (Acts 2:1-4), it has been growing and spreading to the ends of the earth. This expansion will take place until all of God's elect have been reached,

> For this reason I endure all things for the sake of those who are chosen, so that they also may obtain the salvation which is in Christ Jesus *and* with *it* eternal glory (2 Tim 2:10).

At some point in time, when the full measure of God's elect has been drawn to the Messiah, the work of God through the church on the earth will come to its completion. Jesus' Great Commission in Matt 28:19-20 to take the gospel to the ends of the earth will find its fulfillment, as alluded to by the Apostle Paul in Rom 11:25,

> For I do not want you, brethren, to be uninformed of this mystery—so that you will not be wise in your own estimation—that a partial hardening has happened to Israel until the fullness of the Gentiles has come in.

Once the "fullness of the Gentiles" is reached, we can assume that God will take the church to be with Himself and turn His attention to work once again with his people, Israel.

THE END OF THE CHURCH'S EARTHLY SOJOURN

Despite the increasing sinful characteristics of our age, the work of Christ on earth through his church will continue until the moment of his return. In the Great Commission, he promised he would be with us "even to the end of the age" (Matt 28:20). But just as the church had a definite starting point in history, it will also have an ending point of its sojourn on earth. Several Scriptures imply that Christ's second coming was already near or imminent during the time the New Testament was being written:

> Let your gentle spirit be known to all men. The Lord is near (Phil 4:5).
>
> not forsaking our own assembling together, as is the habit of some, but encouraging one another; and all the more as you see the day drawing near (Heb 10:25).
>
> You too be patient; strengthen your hearts, for the coming of the Lord is near (Jas 5:8).
>
> The end of all things is near; therefore, be of sound judgment and sober spirit for the purpose of prayer (1 Pet 4:7).
>
> I am coming quickly; hold fast what you have, so that no one will take your crown (Rev 3:11).

At the end of the Bible, Jesus emphasizes three times that his return is soon:

> And behold, I am coming quickly. Blessed is he who heeds the words of the prophecy of this book (Rev 22:7).
>
> Behold, I am coming quickly, and My reward is with Me (Rev 22:12a).
>
> He who testifies to these things says, "Yes, I am coming quickly." Amen. Come, Lord Jesus (Rev 22:20).

If Christ's return was imminent when those Scriptures were written, then how much nearer must it be today. If the Apostle Paul could write, "...for now salvation is nearer to us than when we believed" (Rom 13:11), then how much closer must it be today? Of course, God does not measure time as we do, for as the Apostle Peter writes, "With the Lord one day is like a thousand years, and a thousand years like one day" (2 Pet 4:8).

Nevertheless, it is true that he could come at any time. There are no prophetic events that must take place before he comes. With this in view, the church has always been exhorted to be spiritually awake and ready for that great event of his appearing (Phil 3:20; 1 Thess 5:1-9).

looking for the blessed hope and the appearing of the glory of our great God and Savior, Christ Jesus (Tit 2:13).

It has always been Christ's aim to have his church in his presence. He first alludes to this in John's Gospel, when he said, "Where I am there my servant will be also" (John 12:26). Later in the same Gospel, Jesus expresses this same desire more fully,

> In My Father's house are many dwelling places; if it were not so, I would have told you; for I go to prepare a place for you. If I go and prepare a place for you, I will come again and receive you to Myself, that where I am, *there* you may be also (John 14:2-3).

This longing to have the church with Him is so strong that He repeats it in his prayer to his Father on behalf of his followers,

> Father, I desire that they also, whom You have given Me, be with Me where I am, so that they may see My glory which You have given Me, for You loved Me before the foundation of the world (John 17:24).

When the church has completed the task of the Great Commission, and God has called his elect to himself from every tribe and nation, then we can assume that Christ will take the church to be with himself. The actual event is revealed in 1 Thess 4:15-17,

> For this we say to you by the word of the Lord, that we who are alive and remain until the coming of the Lord, will not precede those who have fallen asleep. For the

> Lord Himself will descend from heaven with a shout, with the voice of *the* archangel and with the trumpet of God, and the dead in Christ will rise first. Then we who are alive and remain will be caught up together with them in the clouds to meet the Lord in the air, and so we shall always be with the Lord.

Those believers who have died, since the beginning of the church to the time of the rapture, will be raised first, then those believers alive on the earth at the time of that event will be translated to join them, and together the entire church will be brought into Christ's presence. Other verses from Paul supplement this teaching on the resurrection of the church:

> Behold, I tell you a mystery; we will not all sleep, but we will all be changed, in a moment, in the twinkling of an eye, at the last trumpet; for the trumpet will sound, and the dead will be raised imperishable, and we will be changed. (1 Cor 15:51-52).

The apostle also indicates that God will do this through his divine omnipotence:

> For our citizenship is in heaven, from which also we eagerly wait for a Savior, the Lord Jesus Christ; who will transform the body of our humble state into conformity with the body of His glory, by the exertion of the power that He has even to subject all things to Himself (Phil 3:20-21).

The power of God will instantly change us, "in the twinkling of an eye," and will transform us to be like Jesus in his resurrection body:

> Beloved, now we are children of God, and it has not appeared as yet what we will be. We know that when He

> appears, we will be like Him, because we will see Him just as He is (1 John 3:2).

In that instant the church will stand before Christ without any blemish. He will "present to Himself the church in all her glory, having no spot or wrinkle or any such thing…holy and blameless" (Eph 5:27). Jude confirms this amazing truth,

> Now to Him who is able to keep you from stumbling, and to make you stand in the presence of His glory blameless with great joy (Jude 24).

The Scriptures do not reveal when the translation of the church will take place, but we do know that all those chosen of God will come to saving faith, and the church will reach its completion when "the fullness of the Gentiles has come in" (Rom 11:25; 2 Tim 2:10).

Some expositors hold that the church age will come to a close at the end of a period of tribulation when Christ returns to earth; others believe that the church will be removed before the worst part of that tribulation, and still others maintain Christ will rescue and retrieve his church from the earth before that period of judgment commences. All of the major views on the rapture of the church center on their relationship to what is called "the Day of the Lord," sometimes referred to as the tribulation period. This is a period at the end of the current age in which God pours out his judgment (s) on a Christ-rejecting world as specifically chronicled in Rev 6–18, culminating in the second coming of Christ to earth (Rev 19).

The various stances concerning the rapture of the Church have led many to avoid the subject altogether. They do so, either because they have no clarity on the subject or because they feel that taking a position on this topic is unprofitable and only leads to divisions among believers. After being popularized in the 1970s and unfortunately sensationalized in some writings, the topic of the rapture began to fall on hard times. However, since Christ's coming for his church is scriptural and is, as Paul refers to it, "the blessed hope" (Tit 2:13), it is a teaching important to our faith and worthy of serious thought. Therefore, I would like to consider (below) in more detail the major views regarding it.

THE PARTIAL RAPTURE VIEW

A small minority of expositors have argued that the rapture of the church will not include the whole body of Christ. This view maintains that only those who were committed, faithful followers of Christ will be raptured. Those believers who are not taken will be left to be purified in the tribulation period. Some who hold this view cite Heb 9:28 as their Scriptural support. The verse states:

> so Christ also, having been offered once to bear the sins of many, will appear a second time for salvation without *reference to* sin, *to those who eagerly await Him* (emphasis added).

The argument that some believers will not be raptured is based upon the interpretation that Christ is coming only for "those who eagerly await Him." Proponents of this viewpoint add that there are exhortations in the New Testament for believers to watch, pray, remain faithful, and be ready for Christ's coming but not all believers are spiritually ready for this great event. Rather, some will be ashamed at Christ's coming (1 John 2:28). In addition, they argue that in the letters to the seven churches in Rev 2–3, the promise of reward is only made to those who overcome. Enoch is cited as a positive Old Testament example of one who was taken to be with God because he "walked with God" (Gen 5:24). The implication, according to this view, is that those who are not walking closely with God will not experience the rapture.

The main problem with the partial rapture view is that it is based on the good works and faithfulness of the believer, not the promise of God. What about those believers who had already died but in their earthly life had not waited expectantly for his return? Would they also not be resurrected in the rapture? In the New Testament, Christ's gathering of his church to himself is never promised only to those who are spiritual or faithful enough, but rather to all those who are "in Christ," that is, the whole church, both the living and those who have already died (1 Thess 4:13-17). Nor does the New Testament present two resurrections for the church, one for the faithful and a later one for the unfaithful. It seems more likely that a believer's spiritual lethargy and disobedience will be addressed either through God's discipline or loss of reward rather than being left behind at the rapture. Thus, the partial rapture view does not have strong biblical or logical support. Both the living and the dead "in Christ" will be taken in this momentous event. Now let's consider the three major views on the relationship of the rapture to the "Day of the Lord."

THE POST-TRIBULATIONAL PERSPECTIVE ON THE RAPTURE

This view holds that the rapture takes place at the second coming of Christ to the earth. It is simultaneous with the Second Advent. Adherents of this perspective offer several arguments to support their position.

First, advocates maintain that it has been the orthodox belief throughout church history. In that regard, it is considered a tenet of orthodoxy. They argue that separating the rapture from the second coming was a development of later church history.

Second, they argue that those passages that speak of the rapture and those that refer to the second coming employ similar language because they are describing the same event. The words *appearing*, *coming*, *revelation*, and *near* occur in passages that deal with both the rapture and the second coming (cf. Matt 24:27; Rom 13:11-12; 1 Cor 1:7; 1 Thess 4:15-18; 2 Thess 2:8; Titus 2:13; Jas 5:7-8; 1 Pet 1:13; 4:7; Rev 1:3,7; 16:15; 22:7, 12). In addition, exhortations such as *be ready, be sober, be on the alert, wait for, keep awake, and expect* apply to both the rapture and the second coming (cf. Matt 24:42-44; Mark 13:33-37; Luke 12:37, 39-40; 21:36; 1 Thess 5:3-8; 1 Pet 1:13; 4:7; Rev 1:3,7; 16:15; 22:7, 12). Therefore, supporters of this view maintain that these exhortations must allude to the same event.

Third, many post-tribulation adherents equate the rapture in 1 Cor 15:50-55 and 1 Thess 4:13-17 with the resurrection cited in Rev 20:4. They also identify the elect in Matt 24:22 as the church which is present in the period of the tribulation, but just as Israel was protected in Egypt from the plagues, so the church will be present on earth during that period but protected from God's wrath.

Finally, those who hold this view maintain that they still can believe in the imminency of Christ's coming, that is, he could come at any time. They interpret the nearness of Christ's coming (immanency) not to mean that he could come at any moment but rather that his return could take place in any particular generation. Though the post-tribulational view of the rapture has been gaining in popularity and has many adherents, some have challenged this perspective. Here are the main counter-arguments:

First, it is not undisputed that the post-tribulational view of the rapture has been the orthodox view of the church throughout its history. In certain periods of church history, it has been the more popular view, but it is also true that periodically other views have been held. For example, in our own age there is a combination of views on the timing of the rapture.

Second, using similar words and language in describing the rapture and the second coming does point to the fact that the two events share some similarities, but similarity does not necessarily equate them. In fact, there are some differences between the two, most notably, the fact that there are no signs given that precede the rapture, but there are many cataclysmic signs that precede the second coming (cf. John 14:2-3; 1 Cor 15:50-55; 1 Thess 4:13-17; Rev 6–18).

Third, when discussing the Day of the Lord, the period of end-time judgments, Paul clarifies for the Thessalonian church that they were not destined to "wrath" but rather will be "rescued from the wrath to come" (cf. 1 Thess 1:10; 5:2-9. In Rev 6:15-17, the people on earth realize that the "day of wrath" has arrived. By deduction, one can assume the church will not be present for that period, since it is promised to be rescued from those judgments.

Fourth, there are notable distinctions between rapture passages (John 14:2-3; 1 Cor 15:50; 1 Thess 4:13-18) and passages depicting the second coming (2 Thess 1:7-10; Rev 19). The rapture passages are unannounced and instantaneous; the second coming passages are subsequent to a series of distinguishable judgments, visible to the whole earth, and involve some time. In addition, the resurrection in Rev 20:4 after the judgments and second coming is said to precede a thousand-year period. John does not say the church is resurrected at that particular point, but rather those who did not worship the beast during the tribulation period.

Finally, if the rapture and the resurrection at the second coming were simultaneous, no believers would be left on earth, all having been resurrected to be with Christ. Since several passages indicate that Christ will destroy his enemies at the second coming, there would also be no non-believers left on earth (Matt 13:30, 41-43, 49-50; 24:48-51; 25:30, 45-46; 2 Thess 1:5-10; Rev 19:15, 21). If believers are raptured and Christ's enemies are destroyed, there would then be no humans left on earth, either believing or non-believing, and thus no humans left to enter the thousand-year period in their earthly bodies. Thus, a post-tribulational rapture would seem to necessitate that there will be no earthly millennium inhabited by humans in their natural bodies.

Yet, in just six verses, John mentions the time period of a "thousand years" six times (Rev 20:2-7).

THE MID-TRIBULATIONAL OR PRE-WRATH PERSPECTIVE ON THE RAPTURE

The mid-tribulational or pre-wrath view holds that the rapture comes after the judgments in the book of Revelation commence, but before God pours out his wrath at the very end. With this view, there are differing thoughts on when exactly the church will be taken to be with Christ. Some place the rapture at the seventh trumpet of Rev 11:15, "Then the seventh angel sounded." This trumpet comes after the mid-point of the tribulation period. Some also equate that trumpet with the last trumpet of 1 Cori 15:52, which signals the rapture of the church, "In a moment, in the twinkling of an eye, at the last trumpet; for the trumpet will sound, and the dead will be raised imperishable, and we will be changed."

Others have interpreted the resurrection of the two witnesses in Rev 11:11 with the rapture. The general argument is that God did not remove Israel from the plagues that he poured out on Egypt, but rather He protected them in the midst of those judgments. Similarly, God will leave his church on earth during the first part of the Day of the Lord when he pours out judgments on the earth. They also maintain that God would not pour out his wrath on his bride, the church; so, before the period of God's wrath near the end of the tribulation, God will remove the church by means of the rapture.

A counter-argument to this view has been that it falsely interprets the first six seal judgments as not being part of God's wrath. Revelation 6:16-17, looking back on the first six judgments, states, "For the great day of their wrath has come." So if the church is present for the first six judgments, then God's church is experiencing the initial phases of God's judgment and wrath being poured out on the earth. Moreover, there are many trumpet soundings in the Bible. The seventh trumpet of Rev 11:15 is a trumpet of severe judgment and should be distinguished from the trumpet of 1 Cor 15:52 which is not a trumpet of judgment or wrath but rather a trumpet of deliverance and departure, signaling the rapture of the church, which Paul calls "the blessed hope" (Tit 2:13). In addition, there is nothing in the resurrection of the two witnesses of Rev 11:11 that ties that event to the rapture. There is no mention of a trumpet, and the people of earth are actually able to view the physical ascension of the two witnesses. By way of contrast, there is no indication that the non-believing world will be able to see the departure of those raptured. Rather, "in the twinkling of an eye," the believing church will be taken to be with Christ (1 Cor 15:52). It will be similar to Enoch's experience, "Enoch walked with God; and he was not, for God took him" (Gen 5:24). The writer of Hebrews confirms this, "By faith Enoch was taken up so that he would not see death; and he was not found because God took him up" (Heb 11:5). For these reasons, the pre-wrath view has not been as popular as pre- or post-tribulationalism.

THE PRE-TRIBULATIONAL PERSPECTIVE ON THE RAPTURE

Those who hold to a pre-tribulational rapture believe it could occur at any time during the church age (it is imminent) but will occur before the tribulation (that is, at least seven years before the return of Christ to earth). This view has been popular among many dispensational theologians, but in the last few decades has been more vehemently challenged. Those who challenge the view cite some of the arguments already mentioned above in the post-tribulational view of the rapture. In my discussions with some believers who reject this view, they have basically asked, why would God have allowed so many of his children to have suffered and even to have been martyred throughout church history, but then rescue this one generation from such a fate? He didn't remove Israel from Egypt before the ten plagues; why would he remove his church before the Day of the Lord? In addition, many who oppose this view have characterized it as overly sensational or as a "pie-in-the-sky" belief. Yet, there is no reason why it should be considered more sensational than a mid- or post-tribulational rapture. A rapture at any time would be miraculous. We should keep in mind that the determination on whether or not such a view is plausible should not be based on whether or not it appeals to us, but rather on whether or not the Scripture provides ample evidence for it. Adherents to this view put forth several of the following arguments to support it.

Basic to the pre-tribulational view is the observation that at the rapture, Jesus does not descend to the earth, but rather the church is taken up to be with him. In 1 Thess 4, a central rapture passage, those believers who have already died will be raised first, then the remaining church alive on earth will be taken up or "caught up" to meet Christ in the air,

> Then we who are alive and remain will be caught up together with them in the clouds to meet the Lord in the air, and so we shall always be with the Lord (1 Thess 4:17).

By way of contrast, at the second coming is an event visible to all in which the Lord descends to earth, specifically the Mount of Olives (Zech 14:3-4; Matt 24:30; 25:31-33; Acts 1:11; Rev 19:11-21).

Perhaps most central to this view of the rapture is the belief that God has distinctive programs for Israel and the church. In the book of Daniel, the prophet lays out a detailed prophecy regarding God's plan for the redemption of the nation of Israel (Dan 9:24-27). The plan consists of seventy sevens, sometimes called *the seventy-weeks of Daniel.* These weeks are interpreted as year-weeks, that is, each week represents seven years. Thus, the whole period would be the sum of seventy sevens, which is 490 years of tribulation.[7] Pre-tribulationalists believe that the first sixty-nine sevens of Daniel's prophecy have been completed in biblical history. The seventieth seven or last seven-year period is yet future and corresponds to the judgments of the tribulation as recorded in Rev 6–19. All of the seventy weeks apply specifically to the nation of Israel, for the angel Gabriel speaking to Daniel indicated that they referred to, "your people and your city." (Dan 9:24). Since God has distinct plans and purposes for the church and Israel, and since the church was not part of the first sixty-nine weeks of Daniel's prophecy, it is deduced that it will also not be part of the seventieth week. The first sixty-nine weeks are comprised of 483 Jewish years, 360 days each, stretching from the Decree of Artaxerxes to rebuild Jerusalem after the Babylonian captivity in 445 bc to the cutting off of the Messiah in ca. ad 32 (Neh 2:1-4; Dan 9:24-26). The last week of Daniel's prophecy (seven years) also relates to Israel and is determined to be still future.

A second argument for the pre-tribulational view of the rapture is that the New Testament writers believed that the coming of the Lord was close at hand, that is, it could occur at any time (Rom 13:11; Phil 4:5; Jas 5:7-9; Rev 22:7, 12, 20). But, if the rapture were to take place in the middle of the tribulation or at Christ's second coming to earth, the rapture could not be near, for a period of judgment would need to first occur. In addition, there is no mention of the church in the book of Revelation between chapters 6–19 (the tribulation period), though it is mentioned seven times in chapters 2–3 before the judgments begin, and some would argue it is also alluded to as the "bride" after the judgments have ended (Rev 19:7; 21:9; 22:17).

---

7 Since this point requires a more detailed clarification, the reader is encouraged to see the appendix for a more thorough explanation.

Third, most pre-tribulationalists hold that the restrainer of evil, mentioned in 2 Thess 2:7, is the Holy Spirit, since ultimately God alone is able to restrain evil. Paul states, "he who now restrains" will be removed before the Anti-Christ comes. Since the Holy Spirit indwells the church, his removal would imply the church's removal from the earth. This does not mean that the Holy Spirit would no longer be in the world, for He is omnipresent. But it does mean that the rapture of the church will be the elimination of one of God's major means of restraining evil, for the church is presently "the salt of the earth," "the light of the world," and "the pillar and support of the truth" (Matt 5:13-14; 1 Tim 3:15). This point is supported by the promise Christ made to the church in Philadelphia to keep them from the hour of testing that was coming upon the whole world (Rev 3:10). Never has an hour of testing come upon the *whole* world (emphasis mine), thus it is surmised that it is yet future. One explanation is that the keeping "from" or out of this hour alludes to the fact that Christ will remove his church from the earth before that hour begins. By way of summary, this point maintains that the church age began at Pentecost (Acts 2:1-4). Christ sent the Holy Spirit to indwell and unify both Jew and Gentile believers in one body. In John 14:2-3, he promised to come to take the church out of the world to be with him. Thus, the church age will end when the Holy Spirit, the restrainer of evil, is removed (2 Thess 2:7). Since he is indwelling the church, he will, at that time, remove the church from the world, keeping it from the hour of testing, the tribulation period.

Yet another related argument for the pre-tribulational view is that Paul, in his letter to the Thessalonians, tells them, "God has not destined us to wrath" but rather will rescue us from "the wrath to come (1 Thess 1:10; 5:9). The coming period of wrath is often equated with the Day of the Lord, a period referred to by the prophets that commences in Rev 6 (cf. Jer 30:7; Joel 1:15; 2:1, 11, 31; Zeph 1:14; Rev 6:17). Moreover, after teaching about the rapture, Paul says "comfort one another with these words" (1 Thess 4:18). The believer is to be comforted by the thought of the rapture. If we knew that we had to first go through the tribulation period, this would provide little comfort.

Finally, after Christ returns to earth, he will sit on his "glorious throne" (Matt 25:31). He will then separate the sheep from the goats (Matt 25:32-46). But if the rapture were to occur as He descends to the earth (the post-tribulational view), there would be no sheep left on earth to separate from the goats, and no sheep left to populate the millennial kingdom since they would all have been raptured. But if the rapture takes place several (at least seven) years before the actual coming to earth, then during the time after the rapture, multitudes could come to faith, as Rev 7:1-14 says will happen. Then, when Christ returns, he will destroy all his enemies, and those believers who survived the tribulation period will be those sheep who enter the millennial kingdom in their earthly bodies (Matt 13:41-43, 49-50).

The counter-arguments to the pre-tribulational position on the rapture have been presented above in the mid- and post-tribulational discussions. There are, of course, other views regarding the rapture of the church, but these are the main ones.

THE CHURCH WITH CHRIST IN GLORY

Regardless of one's view on the timing of the rapture, the church has, with few exceptions, held that at death the Christian's body goes into the ground, but his or her spirit goes directly to be with the Lord.

> Therefore, being always of good courage, and knowing that while we are at home in the body we are absent from the Lord—for we walk by faith, not by sight—we are of good courage, I say, and prefer rather to be absent from the body and to be at home with the Lord (2 Cor 5:6-8).

> But I am hard-pressed from both *directions*, having the desire to depart and be with Christ, for *that* is very much better (Phil 1:23).

At the coming of Christ for his church, He will bring with Him the spirits of those believers who have died and are with Him in heaven. He will raise their bodies to unite them with their spirits,

> God will bring with Him those who have fallen asleep in Jesus...For the Lord Himself will descend from heaven with a shout, with the voice of *the* archangel and with the trumpet of God, and the dead in Christ will rise first (1 Thess 4:14a, 16).

Those believers who are still living on earth will be instantly transformed and translated into Christ's presence to join the believers who have died in Christ.

> Then we who are alive and remain will be caught up together with them in the clouds to meet the Lord in the air, and so we shall always be with the Lord (1 Thess 4:17).

Thus, the whole church, together in one instant, "in the twinkling of an eye" shall be caught up to meet Christ in the air (1 Cor. 15:50-58). In his letter to the Philippians, Paul makes clear that God will accomplish this miraculous event through his omnipotent power,

> For our citizenship is in heaven, from which also we eagerly wait for a Savior, the Lord Jesus Christ; who will transform the body of our humble state into conformity with the body of His glory, by the exertion of the power that He has even to subject all things to Himself (Phil 3:20-21).

This "blessed hope," as Paul calls it, will be what the church experiences at the rapture. We will be individually, yet corporately, presented without condemnation, faultless and joyful before Christ (cf. Rom 8:1; Tit 2:13; 1 John 3:2).

> That He might present to Himself the church in all her glory, having no spot or wrinkle or any such thing; but that she would be holy and blameless (Eph 5:27).

> Now to Him who is able to keep you from stumbling, and to make you stand in the presence of His glory blameless with great joy (Jude 24).

The church will be transformed and conformed into Christ's image at its translation (Rom 8:29-30). The Apostle John states, "We know that when He appears, we will be like Him, because we will see Him just as He is" (1 John 3:2). At that point, we will have been prepared to see and experience the glory of God forever (John 17:22-24).

THE CHURCH REWARDED

At some point after the church is taken to be with Christ, her labor, that is, her service for Christ, will be appraised by God and rewarded (Eph 6:8; 1 Cor 3:8, 12-15; Rom 14:10, 12; 2 Cor. 5:10).

> For we must all appear before the judgment seat of Christ, so that each one may be recompensed for his deeds in the body, according to what he has done, whether good or bad (2 Cor 5:10).

This will not be a judgment or evaluation of sin, since Christ has already suffered the penalty for our transgressions.

> Truly, truly, I say to you, he who hears My word, and believes Him who sent Me, has eternal life, and does not

> come into judgment, but has passed out of death into life (John 5:24).

> For Christ also died for sins once for all, *the* just for *the* unjust, so that He might bring us to God, having been put to death in the flesh, but made alive in the spirit (1 Pet 3:18).

But rather, it will be an evaluation for reward. The "deeds" that are to be "recompensed" are the labor or good works done in the name of Christ.

Some have argued that serving God out of a motive for reward is unspiritual. But God offers to reward our service for the very purpose of motivating us spiritually to serve him. Denigrating the idea of rewards only hinders a valid means that God has designed to glorify himself and accomplish his work. In addition, it discourages believers from the service to which he has called them. The believer's service for God is so important that he will hold each of his servants accountable for it and reward them accordingly.

Several Scriptures indicate that Christ will consider several different factors when rewarding his church corporately and its members individually. He will evaluate faithfulness, motive in service, sacrifice, and quality of work.

FAITHFULNESS

Faithfulness is perhaps the most important characteristic of our service for Christ that will be evaluated. In the Parable of the Talents, a master leaves on a journey and disperses to his servants talents that he expects them to invest. In the immediate context, the servants were believing followers of the Messiah. Upon the master's return, he evaluates what each servant did with the talents that he had given to them. To those who were responsible and faithful in investing the talents, he says,

> "Well done, good and faithful slave, you were faithful with a few things, I will put you in charge of many things; enter into the joy of your master" (Matt. 25:21, 23).

Their reward will involve increased responsibility when they "enter into the joy of their master." The joy they would experience most likely refers to the servant entering into the kingdom at the second coming of the Messiah (see also Matt 25:1-13). The Apostle Paul addresses the same concept for the church when he writes, "it is required of stewards that one be found trustworthy" or faithful (1 Cor 4:2). God will evaluate and reward our faithfulness in serving him.

HEART-MOTIVE

A second factor that God will take into account when granting rewards to his servants is their heart motive. Jesus had to correct his disciples, James and John, when they sought positions of personal greatness in his coming kingdom. They asked to sit on Jesus' left and right in glory. This was probably a request for Jesus to grant them the highest ruling positions in his government whenever he would begin his rule. Their motives were self-serving. Jesus had to clarify that seeking reward for personal status, position, or self-aggrandizement is misguided and contrary to Christ's kingdom values (Mark 10:35-45). Rather, service must derive from a pure heart, not seeking one's own glory but rather seeking to do God's will. Paul makes this point clear when addressing slaves in Ephesians,

> not by way of eyeservice, as men-pleasers, but as slaves of Christ, doing the will of God from the heart. With good will render service, as to the Lord, and not to men, knowing that whatever good thing each one does, this he will receive back from the Lord, whether slave or free (Eph. 6:6-8).

In Colossians, Paul refers to the correct motive for service as "sincerity of heart" (Col 3:22). But he more thoroughly reveals the deep nature of God's evaluation of our motives for service in his first letter to the Corinthian church.

> In this case, moreover, it is required of stewards that one be found trustworthy. But to me it is a very small thing that I may be examined by you, or by *any* human court; in fact, I do not even examine myself. For I am conscious of nothing against myself, yet I am not by this acquitted; but the one who examines me is the Lord. Therefore do not go on passing judgment before the time, *but wait* until the Lord comes who will both bring to light the things hidden in the darkness and disclose the motives of *men's* hearts; and then each man's praise will come to him from God (1 Cor 4:2-5).

In that passage, Paul refers both to motive in service and the fact of future reward in the words, "then each man's praise will come to him from God." Apparently, even the smallest act of kindness will be rewarded by God, "For truly, I say to you, whoever gives you a cup of water to drink because you belong to Christ will by no means lose his reward" (Mark 9:41).

SACRIFICE, SUFFERING, AND MARTYRDOM

During his earthly ministry, Jesus addressed the truth that God would at some point reward those who sacrificed on his behalf. He first brought this up when answering Peter's question about what he and the other disciples could expect from God for the sacrifices they had already made in leaving their vocations to follow him. Jesus answered,

> Truly, say to you that you who have followed Me, in the regeneration when the Son of Man will sit on His

> glorious throne, you also shall sit upon twelve thrones, judging the twelve tribes of Israel. And everyone who has left houses or brothers or sisters or father or mother or children or farms for My name's sake, will receive many times as much, and will inherit eternal life." (Matt 19:28-29).

The Apostle Paul also expresses this principle when he writes, "For I consider that the sufferings of this present time are not worthy to be compared with the glory that is to be revealed to us" (Rom 8:18). Similarly, he writes in 2 Corinthians, "For this light momentary affliction is preparing for us an eternal weight of glory beyond all comparison" (2 Cor 4:17). In other words, the temporal sacrifices made will pale in comparison to the eternal joy and glory that will be experienced when God rewards his servants. Paul was not alone in referring to this. The Apostle Peter also wrote about the future reward for the believer who has endured suffering,

> So that the tested genuineness of your faith—more precious than gold that perishes though it is tested by fire—may be found to result in praise and glory and honor at the revelation of Jesus Christ" (1 Pet 1:7).

Later in the same epistle, he pens these words,

> Beloved, do not be surprised at the fiery ordeal among you, which comes upon you for your testing, as though some strange thing were happening to you; but to the degree that you share the sufferings of Christ, keep on rejoicing, so that also at the revelation of His glory you may rejoice with exultation (1 Pet 4:12-13).

In the last book of the Bible, martyrs are promised great blessings for their sufferings,

> Be faithful until death, and I will give you the crown of life (Rev 2:10).

> And I heard a voice from heaven, saying, "Write, Blessed are the dead who die in the Lord from now on! Yes," says the Spirit, "so that they may rest from their labors, for their deeds follow with them" (Rev 14:13).

God will not be outdone; there is no suffering that we may experience for his sake that he will not abundantly and graciously recompense.

QUALITY OF LABOR

Perhaps the most explicit teaching on the importance of the quality of our labor for the Lord is found in 1 Cor 3. Paul first cites the general principle that God will recompense his servants according to their labor, "Now he who plants and he who waters are one; but each will receive his own reward according to his own labor" (1 Cor 3:8). Then, getting more specific, the apostle reveals the thorough evaluation that God will apply to our work,

> Now if any man builds on the foundation with gold, silver, precious stones, wood, hay, straw, each man's work will become evident; for the day will show it because it is *to be* revealed with fire, and the fire itself will test the quality of each man's work. If any man's work which he has built on it remains, he will receive a reward. If any man's work is burned up, he will suffer loss; but he himself will be saved, yet so as through fire (1 Cor 3:12-15).

These are the major criteria that God will take into consideration when rewarding his servants for their labor. As seen in the last verse of the above citation, these works have nothing to do with our salvation, but rather they have to do with our post-salvation service (Eph 2:8-10). It must be added that apart from our labor and rewards earned, God has the prerogative and right to reward believers out of his pure grace. This was made clear in a parable given by Jesus about laborers in the vineyard. At the end of the parable, the landowner representing God says, "Is it not lawful for me to do what I wish with what is my own?" (Matt 20:15a). In addition, there may be a corporate or communal sense in which the church as a whole is rewarded. Just as in the case of the employment of spiritual gifts, "if *one* member is honored, all the members rejoice with it," so too at the time of reward it may be that all will share in the joy of what God accomplished though his church (1 Cor 12:26b). For example, Paul writes to the Thessalonians, "For who is our hope or joy or crown of exultation? Is it not even you, in the presence of our Lord Jesus at His coming?" (1 Thess 2:19). In that statement we see that the apostle expected to share in the future joy of the Thessalonian believers. This is all the more reason that we should rejoice in the success and ministry of others. We may share in their reward!

One way that the New Testament writers address the topic of rewards is through the receiving of specific crowns. For example, there is a crown (reward) for the believer who suffers martyrdom. Paul, knowing he was about to be executed, refers to the crown he and others would receive for suffering imprisonment and ultimately facing martyrdom,

> In the future there is laid up for me the crown of righteousness, which the Lord, the righteous Judge, will award to me on that day; and not only to me, but also to all who have loved His appearing (2 Tim 4:8b).

Notice also that "the crown of righteousness" will also be awarded to "all those who have loved his appearing."

There is also a crown for faithfully enduring trials and persecution,

> Blessed is a man who perseveres under trial; for once he has been approved, he will receive the crown of life which *the Lord* has promised to those who love Him" (Jas 1:12).

There is a reward or crown for faithfully shepherding Christ's flock. In other words, a pastor's painstaking work will find reward,

> And when the Chief Shepherd appears, you will receive the unfading crown of glory (1 Pet 5:4).

There is a reward for believers who faithfully persevere in the faith during difficult times. To the church of Philadelphia, he promises,

> I am coming quickly; hold fast what you have, so that no one will take your crown" (Rev 3:11).

All these different types of crowns allude to God's multifaceted ways of honoring his servants and rewarding his church. Ultimately, even the crowns received will be recognized as gifts of God's grace (Rev 4:4,10-11).

> Around the throne *were* twenty-four thrones; and upon the thrones I *saw* twenty-four elders sitting, clothed in white garments, and golden crowns on their heads...the twenty-four elders will fall down before Him who sits on the throne, and will worship Him who lives forever and ever, and will cast their crowns before the throne, saying, "Worthy are You, our Lord and our God, to receive glory and honor and power; for You created all things, and because of Your will they existed, and were created."

Though most of these crowns (rewards) are due to the struggles and labors that believers endure, they are nevertheless expressions of God's grace. The fact that God will reward his church is emphasized as a valid motivation to serve him in all that we do.

> Therefore, my beloved brethren, be steadfast, immovable, always abounding in the work of the Lord, knowing that your toil is not in vain in the Lord" (1 Cor 15:58).

Once the church is translated and rewarded, Paul reveals that it will then be forever with Christ as expressed by the words, "and so we shall always be with the Lord" (1 Thess 4:17b).

THE CHURCH WITH CHRIST DURING THE 1000 YEARS

Although the church will be taken to be with Christ in the rapture, if it is to "always be with the Lord," as Paul says, then it shall also return with him to take part in his glorious millennial reign on the earth (John 14:2-3; 1 Thess 4:16-17; Rev 5:10). Indeed, this period will be a golden era in which God's people from all the ages take part.

> I say to you that many will come from east and west, and recline at the table with Abraham, Isaac and Jacob in the kingdom of heaven (Matt 8:11).

Matthew refers to this period as the "kingdom of heaven" for it will be a rule on earth in which God's will is done as it is in heaven (Matt 6:10). Among those who take part in this kingdom, the church will have a special role. Paul refers to the Church returning with Christ as "the coming of our Lord Jesus with all His saints" (1 Thess 3:13). Jude refers to it proleptically (as though it was already completed) by stating, "Behold, the Lord came with many thousands of His holy ones" (Jude 14). The Apostle John also describes the event, "And the armies which are in heaven, clothed in fine linen, white *and* clean, were following Him on white horses" (Rev 19:14). The armies in heaven most likely refer to the church, for the clothing of this army is described as "fine linen, white, *and* clean." The same words were used to describe the bride's attire a few verses earlier,

"It was given to her to clothe herself in fine linen, bright *and* clean; for the fine linen is the righteous acts of the saints" (Rev 19:8). Earlier in the book he writes, "those who are with Him [at His coming] *are the* called and chosen and faithful" (Rev 17:14). This means the church (along with a multitude of angels) will return with Christ at his second coming.[8]

If the twelve apostles who were the foundation of the early church are going to rule over the twelve tribes of Israel as Jesus promised them, they will need to experience resurrection and be part of the return and rule of the Messiah on the earth.

> Truly, say to you that you who have followed Me, in the regeneration when the Son of Man will sit on His glorious throne, you also shall sit upon twelve thrones, judging the twelve tribes of Israel (Matt 19:28).

If the "overcomers" that Christ exhorts in his messages to the seven churches are going to rule with him on the earth as he promises, they also will need to return with him (Rev 2:26-27; 5:9-10). The same can be said for the entire body of Christ. If we are to return and rule with Christ, we will need to be resurrected. After declaring that Christ had redeemed men and women from all nations, the Apostle John states,

> You have made them *to be* a kingdom and priests to our God; and they will reign upon the earth (Rev 5:10).

Noteworthy is the location of their reign "upon the earth." One of the many purposes that Christ has for his church in this present era is to prepare us for this future priestly rule. Peter writes that believers comprise a "royal priesthood" (1 Pet 2:5, 9). The Apostle John also expresses the same idea, "He has made us *to be* a kingdom, priests to His God and Father" (Rev 1:6). Christ's

---

8 Myriads of angels will accompany Christ and his church when they come (Matt 16:27; 25:31; 2 Thess 1:7).

mission was to purchase for God with his blood, "*men* from every tribe and tongue and people and nation" so that they would serve him as priests and "reign upon the earth" (Rev 5:9-10).

In addition, once the Messiah has returned to the earth in power and glory, if those Jews who throughout Old Testament history believed in God are going to participate in his kingdom, they also will need to experience resurrection (Ezek 37:1-11; Dan 12:2). The same can be argued for those believers who will be martyrs in the tribulation period (Rev 20:4). The writer of Hebrews may be referring to Old and New Testament saints enjoying the kingdom together when he writes,

> And all these [Old Testament saints], having gained approval through their faith, did not receive what was promised [the kingdom], because God had provided something better for us [who are part of the church], so that apart from us they would not be made perfect [be resurrected] (Heb 11:39-40).

The thousand-year rule of Christ on earth appears to be the venue in which the church and Old Testament believers will together in various capacities co-rule with him. The Apostle Paul believed in this future reality. In correcting the Corinthians who were acting as though they had already become kings, he said, "I wish that you had become kings so that we also might reign with you" (1 Cor 4:8). Paul understood there was a coming future reign for believers and that he and his co-laborers would be part of that rule at the same time the Corinthian believers would. In the letter to the church at Thyatira, Jesus promises this future reign,

> He who overcomes, and he who keeps My deeds until the end, to him I will give authority over the nations; and he shall rule them with a rod of iron, as the vessels of the

> potter are broken to pieces, as I also have received *authority* from My Father (Rev 2:26-27).

In the above quote, John cites an Old Testament messianic text to refer to Christ's reign but applies it to believers in the church (cf. Ps 2:8-9; Rev 2:26-27). Also, to the church of Laodicea, Jesus promises,

> "He who overcomes, I will grant to him to sit down with Me on My throne, as I also overcame and sat down with My Father on His throne" (Rev 3:21).

Notice that Christ distinguishes here between his throne and his Father's throne. He sits on his Father's throne in heaven now (Heb 1:3). But at his second coming he will leave that throne and return to earth to sit on the throne of David, "But when the Son of Man comes in His glory, and all the angels with Him, then He will sit on His glorious throne" (Matt 25:31). Isaiah refers to this as a reign from, "the throne of David and over his kingdom" (Isa 9:7).

> There will be no end to the increase of *His* government or of peace, on the throne of David and over his kingdom, to establish it and to uphold it with justice and righteousness from then on and forevermore. The zeal of the Lord of hosts will accomplish this.

To summarize this point, one of God's purposes for his church is to one day co-rule with their Messiah on the earth. This means that believers in their resurrected bodies will co-mingle with those entering the millennial kingdom in their natural bodies, the believing remnant left alive on the earth at his coming. This arrangement appears improbable to some interpreters, yet Christ in his resurrected body has already provided the precedent for such a scenario. He was in his resurrected body while co-mingling with his disciples in their natural bodies, and this was not thought strange or impossible. Their interaction with one another was normal. Much can be gleaned about the thousand-year kingdom reign of Christ on the earth from the Psalms and Old Testament prophets, but little detail is given to us regarding how the church specifically functions during that time, except to indicate that we will be with him and co-rule as royal priests.

PART V

The Church
IN ETERNITY

Most assuredly, saints of all the ages will share eternity with the church. The church was created ultimately to be with Christ forever, to enjoy and glorify him eternally. The Apostle Paul makes clear that the church was predestined, called, and justified, and will one day also be glorified (Rom 8:30). We will see him in his glory and "be like him" (1 John 3:2). Paul personifies the fallen creation, when he writes, "For the anxious longing of the creation waits eagerly for the revealing of the sons of God" (Rom 8:19). The revealing of the sons of God alludes to the time when God will reveal to the rest of creation the glorified church. Apart from the last two chapters of the Bible, little is written for us regarding the eternal state. However, what is revealed is glorious, guiding our imaginations in how our eternal life will be lived out in his presence. It will be a relationship of joy. The Psalmist writes,

> In Your presence is fullness of joy, in Your right hand there are pleasures forever (Ps 16:11).

We will never again struggle with sin; we will live "holy and blameless before Him" (Eph 1:4). Several glimpses of our eternal life are given to us in the Apostle John's letters to the seven churches. For example, in his encouragement to the church at Ephesus, John writes, "To him who overcomes, I will grant to eat of the tree of life which is in the Paradise of God" (Rev 2:7). This is a reference to the tree of life in the New Jerusalem (Rev 22:2). It may be that God will imbue the fruit on the tree of life with the power to energize and sustain eternal life much the way food in our current order sustains our life on earth. This promise is akin to the promise of eternal life itself.

To the church at Smyrna, Christ promises "the crown of life," which is also a reference to eternal life. He assures them that they will not be hurt by the second death, which will take place at the great white throne judgment (cf. Rev 2:10-11; 20:11-15).

To the church of Pergamum, he promises "hidden manna," possibly an allusion to the sustenance of eternal life, or the bread of life which came down from heaven, Jesus himself (John 6:51).

> He who has an ear, let him hear what the Spirit says to the churches. To him who overcomes, to him I will give some of the hidden manna, and I will give him a white stone, and a new name written on the stone which no one knows but he who receives it (Rev 2:17).

The Spirit also promises them a new name, which signifies that in the New Jerusalem we will experience our new identity in Christ completely. It is interesting to think that we will be so totally changed that we no longer go by the name our parents gave us, but rather by a new name given to us by the Lord. The promised white stone and new name signify that we have been granted release from death (Rev 2:17). Some maintain that in the ancient world a white stone was given to those prisoners on death row who had been acquitted. Others hold that it was given to athletes who won a contest.

The risen Christ promises the church of Thyatira "the morning star," which at the end of the book he describes as "the bright morning star" (Rev 2:26-28; 22:). The Apostle Peter refers to it as something like an inner light shining in our hearts (2 Pet 1:19).

To the church at Sardis, Christ promises white garments depicting a state of holiness that cannot and will not be lost. Also, he grants us assurance that our names will never be erased from the book of life, and confidence that Christ will forever represent us before the Father (Rev 3:4-5).

To the church of Philadelphia, he promises that they will be a "pillar." In other words, believers will have a stable standing before God forever. In addition, He promises that we will never depart from God. He will have written on us the name of God and the New Jerusalem, signifying that we belong totally and forever to him (Rev 3:11-12).

Finally, to the church of Laodicea, Christ promises them the right to sit on his throne with him. That speaks of their co-rulership with Him forever (Rev 3:21). All of these promises to the churches characterize the life believers will enjoy in eternity.

Paul writes that we will be released from the death and corruption of the old (first) creation and enter into a glorious new reality,

> The creation itself also will be set free from its slavery to corruption into the freedom of the glory of the children of God" (Rom 8:21).

Though this new order may refer to the creation of the new heaven and earth, (Rev 21:1), it is also possible that Paul is referring to the new order that will be established at the second coming of Christ and the establishment of the millennial kingdom, for the children of God will so-to-speak shed their mortal coil and enter into glory at the rapture of the church when "we will see him just as he is" (cf. 1 Thess 4:16-17; 1 John 3:2). The Apostle John, however, definitely refers to the new creation when he writes,

> And I heard a loud voice from the throne, saying, "Behold, the tabernacle of God is among men, and He will dwell among them, and they shall be His people, and God

> Himself will be among them, and He will wipe away every tear from their eyes; and there will no longer be *any* death; there will no longer be *any* mourning, or crying, or pain; the first things have passed away" (Rev 21:3-4).

We will experience these conditions with him in the new heaven and new earth, and in the new Jerusalem (Rev 21:1-2). For all the ages of eternity, the church will be a trophy and testimony of God's grace to be marveled at by men and angels. It will uniquely reveal his wisdom and the riches of his glory (Rom 9:23; Eph 3:10). All his creation will marvel at the abundant mercy and sublime grace that God has displayed in redeeming and transforming his church forever,

> so that in the ages to come He might show the surpassing riches of His grace in kindness toward us in Christ Jesus (Eph 2:7).

We will be co-heirs with Christ, which means that he will share with us all that he has inherited from his Father (Rom 8:17; Eph 1:11; 1 Pet 1:3-4; Rev 21:7). The place of our eternal residence with Christ is called the new Jerusalem. Its dimensions and the glory of its precious foundation stones are staggering (Rev 21:10-23). In addition, its life-giving river and its "tree of life" are readily accessible.

We need not worry that there will ever be a moment of boredom. Rather, we will be continually thrilled. As cited above, "In Your presence is fullness of joy, in Your right hand there are pleasures forever" (Ps 16:11). Most glorious of all will be life in the presence of the Lamb:

> There will no longer be any curse; and the throne of God and of the Lamb will be in it [the new Jerusalem], and His bond-servants will serve Him; they will see His face, and His name *will be* on their foreheads. And there will

> no longer be *any* night; and they will not have need of the light of a lamp nor the light of the sun, because the Lord God will illumine them; and they will reign forever and ever (Rev 22:3-5).

Jesus' commentary on all this is, "He who overcomes will inherit these things" (Rev 21:7). In short, the purpose of the church in eternity future will be to enjoy and glorify God forever. Our destiny will be "to the praise of His glory" (Eph 1:6, 12, 14).

> Now to Him who is able to do far more abundantly beyond all that we ask or think, according to the power that works within us, to Him *be* the glory in the church and in Christ Jesus to all generations forever and ever. Amen (Eph 3:20-21).

CONCLUSION,

In *The Church in God's Eternal Plan*, I have argued that the church is a unique and special work of God. God envisioned it in eternity past; it had a starting point in history, a purpose in its earthly sojourn, and a completion that is yet future. It also has a millennial purpose, and even more importantly, an eternal purpose in the New Jerusalem.

The church is a distinctive work of God in his eternal plan, so-to-speak a precious jewel of great worth, yet as we experience it today, a diamond in the rough. Even so, it exists as a cosmic revelation of God's grace, destined to share in Christ's glory. We who comprise the church are a precious gift that God the Father is preparing and planning to present to his beloved Son (cf. John 6:37; 17:2, 6, 9).

Father, I desire that they also, whom You have given Me, be with Me where I am (John 17:24).

APPENDIX

THE CHURCH AND THE SEVENTY WEEKS OF DANIEL

Here, I would like to offer a more detailed explanation of Dan 9:24-27, popularly called *the seventy weeks of Daniel.* The prophet lays out a detailed prophecy regarding God's plan for the redemption of the nation of Israel. The seventy-year captivity in Babylon was coming to an end, and Daniel was praying for his nation. The angel Gabriel was sent to explain to him God's plan for the completion of Israel's salvation. Gabriel says that seventy weeks (lit. *seventy-sevens*) have been determined by God to finish his purpose and plan for the redemption of the nation. These were not seventy literal weeks, for God did not finish his plan in that time. Also, when Daniel used the term "weeks" to refer to normal weeks of seven days, he said so. For example, in Dan 10:2, he writes that he had been mourning for "three weeks." The Hebrew literally reads, "three sevens of days."[9] In Dan 9:24, the English word "weeks" does not occur in the Hebrew text. Literally, it says, "seventy sevens," but he does not qualify the phrase with the word "days." Rather, it is seventy units of seven, or 490, increments in total.

> Seventy weeks [lit. "sevens"] have been decreed for your people [Israel] and your holy city [Jerusalem], to finish the transgression, to make an end of sin, to make atonement

9 It is also helpful to observe the use of the word "seven" in the story of Nebuchadnezzar's period of insanity. He was to be driven away for a period of "seven times" (Dan 4:23, 25, 32). It could not have referred to seven days, for in the time period indicated his hair had grown to be like eagles' feathers and his nails like birds' claws. Also, seven months may not have been long enough for his nails to grow as long a birds' claws. It is not implausible that "seven times" referred to a period of seven years.

> for iniquity, to bring in everlasting righteousness, to seal up vision and prophecy and to anoint the most holy *place* (Dan 9:24).

By looking at the start and end events of the first sixty-nine increments (that is, the first seven increments plus sixty-two increments), we can determine how long each period was. Notice that Daniel says the issuing of a decree begins the seventy weeks.

> So you are to know and discern *that* from the issuing of a decree to restore and rebuild Jerusalem until Messiah the Prince *there will be* seven weeks and sixty-two weeks; it will be built again, with plaza and moat, even in times of distress (Dan 9:25).

The first historical event begins with the decree to rebuild Jerusalem. There are several decrees given in the book of Ezra, but none of them deal directly with the rebuilding of the city of Jerusalem. For example, Cyrus' decree (539 bc) allowed the Jews to return to their land to rebuild the temple, but no authority was given to rebuild the city of Jerusalem (Ezra 1:1-3). However, in Nehemiah, King Artaxerxes gave a decree in 444 bc that allowed Nehemiah to return from Persia to Jerusalem to rebuild the city walls (Neh 2:4-8). This decree seems to fit best what Daniel described (Dan 9:25). According to the angel's revelation, the Messiah would arrive and mark the end of the sixty-ninth increment. Then, after these sixty-nine periods conclude, two things will happen: the Messiah will be cut off and the city of Jerusalem, including the temple, will be destroyed. Jesus was crucified in ca. ad 32, and historically we know that Jerusalem, along with its temple, was destroyed by the Romans in ad 70. Both of those events, the cutting off of the Messiah (his crucifixion) and the destruction of the city, would take place after the sixty-ninth increment ended but before the seventieth increment began.

> Then after the sixty-two weeks [that is the seven plus sixty-two increments] the Messiah will be cut off and have nothing, and the people of the prince who is to come will destroy the city and the sanctuary. And its end *will come* with a flood; even to the end there will be war; desolations are determined (Dan 9:26).

This means the sixty-nine increments started in 444 bc and ended in ad 32 before the crucifixion. This equals 476 years (Gregorian years of 365 days), there being only one year between 1 bc and ad 1. However, the Jewish year consisted of 360 days or twelve months of thirty days each instead of 365 days as our years do.[10] By using this Jewish reckoning of 360 days in a year, we can determine that the sixty-nine increments of seven (476 of our Gregorian years) actually add up to 483 Jewish years. From Nehemiah's decree in 444 bc to the cutting off of the Messiah in ad 32 is 476 Gregorian years, or 483 Jewish years. By dividing the 483 Jewish years by the sixty-nine increments, we can determine the length of a single increment, which is seven Jewish years. This leaves just one increment of time left, the seventieth increment, sometimes referred to as the seventieth week of Daniel. According to this unit of time, that last increment would be seven Jewish years of 360 days each.

History tells us that the first sixty-nine increments have already taken place. The Messiah was cut off after the sixty-ninth week was complete, yet before the seventieth or last week began. The last increment of seven years will start when a certain

10 This can be determined by observing how Moses calculated the days of the Genesis flood (Gen 6–9). The Flood began in the six-hundredth year of Noah's life, specifically on the seventeenth day of the second month of that year (Gen 7:11). The Flood ended on the seventeenth day of the seventh month (Gen 8:4). Thus, it lasted exactly five months. Moses says these five months consisted of exactly "one hundred and fifty days" (Gen 7:24; 8:3). From this we can observe that each month had a length of thirty days. Thus, twelve months of thirty days each equals a year consisting of 360 days. Supporting this calculation are the 42 months mentioned in Rev 11:2, which are expressed as 1260 days in Rev 11:3. This would be 42 months of 30 days each.

"prince" (Dan 9:26) signs a one-week (literally, *one seven*) covenant with Israel.

> And he ["the prince who is to come, v. 26] will make a firm covenant with the many for one week [one increment of seven] (Dan 9:27a).

Such a covenant has not yet been made with Israel, but when it is, it will be a covenant for seven (Jewish) years. By interpreting this prophecy in this way, we can see that there is an undetermined gap of time between the end of the sixty-ninth week and the start of the seventieth week. Daniel has already mentioned two events that took place in that gap: the cutting off of the Messiah and the destruction of the city of Jerusalem. The seventieth week (or seventieth increment) will begin when the prince to come makes a covenant with Israel. Many believe this refers to the future Antichrist. Most pre-tribulationalists equate this last seven-year period with the tribulation of Rev 6–19.

Though these calculations have been detailed, we don't want to *miss the forest for the trees.* The main point of this for the argument of a pre-tribulational rapture is that that the church was not part of the first sixty-nine weeks of Daniel's prophecy from Nehemiah's decree to Christ's crucifixion (for the church did not come into existence until Acts 2), therefore it is inferred that it also will not be part of the future seventieth week (the final seven years) because Daniel was told that the whole period of seventy sevens was designated specifically for "your people and your holy city," that is the nation of Israel and Jerusalem respectively—not the church!

> Seventy weeks have been decreed for your people [Israel] and your holy city [Jerusalem]...(Dan 9:24a).

Thus, it is deduced that God's calendar for Israel and his purpose for the church are distinct. The church was not present for the first sixty-nine increments of Daniel's prophecy; it will also not be present in the seventieth increment, otherwise known as the tribulation period.[11]

11 The first sixty-nine weeks belonged to Israel, not the church. The same is the case for the seventieth week, it relates to Israel, not the church. Thus, expositors holding to a pre-tribulational perspective argue that the church is not part of the seventieth week of Daniel 9:27. It is surmised that the church age will end before the seventieth week (the last seven-year period) of Daniel 9:27 begins. Those who hold this viewpoint maintain that this period of seven years in Daniel's seventieth week harmonizes with the time indicators recorded for the judgments in Revelation 6-18. John breaks down the period into two sections of three- and-a-half-years each (Rev 11:2, 3; 12:6; 13:5).

ALSO AVAILABLE FROM LAMPION HOUSE PUBLISHING

FOREWORD BY
E.D. HIRSCH, JR.

The THEORY & PRACTICE of *Biblical* HERMENEUTICS:
ESSAYS IN HONOR OF ELLIOTT E. JOHNSON

H. WAYNE HOUSE
FORREST S. WEILAND
EDITORS

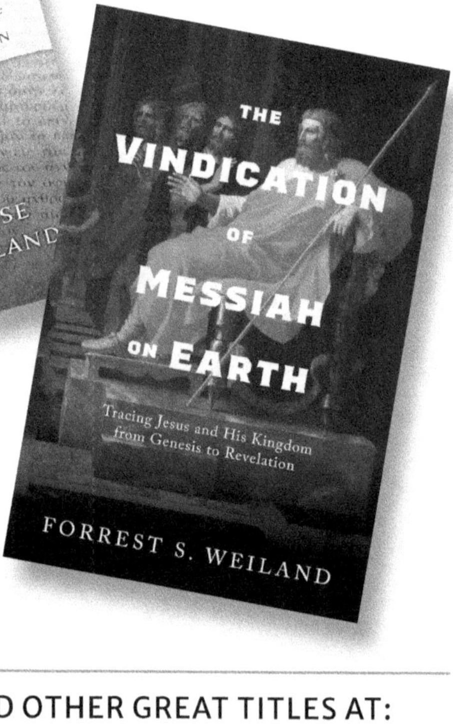

THE VINDICATION OF MESSIAH ON EARTH
Tracing Jesus and His Kingdom from Genesis to Revelation

FORREST S. WEILAND

LOOK FOR THESE AND OTHER GREAT TITLES AT:

LAMPIONHOUSEPUBLISHING.COM

www.ingramcontent.com/pod-product-compliance
Lightning Source LLC
LaVergne TN
LVHW010840120826
845149LV00017B/3331
9798991827843